SpringerBriefs in Computer Science

T0213815

More information about this series at http://www.springer.com/series/10028

Márcio Ribeiro · Paulo Borba
Claus Brabrand

Emergent Interfaces for Feature Modularization

 Springer

Márcio Ribeiro
Computing Institute
Federal University of Alagoas
Maceió, Alagoas
Brazil

Claus Brabrand
Department of Software and Systems
IT University of Copenhagen
Copenhagen
Denmark

Paulo Borba
Informatics Center
Federal University of Pernambuco
Recife
Brazil

ISSN 2191-5768   ISSN 2191-5776 (electronic)
ISBN 978-3-319-11492-7 ISBN 978-3-319-11493-4 (eBook)
DOI 10.1007/978-3-319-11493-4

Library of Congress Control Number: 2014951726

Springer Cham Heidelberg New York Dordrecht London

Printed on acid-free paper

Springer is part of Springer Science+Business Media (www.springer.com)

To our families

Foreword

Software systems in a wide range of domains need to be increasingly configurable. Program families and software product lines are well-known forms of configurable software systems. Companies are often launching initiatives and new projects involving configurable software systems, as they enable organizations to achieve time-to-market gains and cost reductions. These systems are often decomposed into a set of features, which represent semantically cohesive units of behavior. Features describe the commonalities and variabilities of programs potentially derived from a configurable software system.

Unfortunately, developers still struggle to properly maintain the source code of software families and product lines. These systems typically have many features, and each feature may have from dozens to thousands of lines of code. The implementation of each feature is often scattered through the modules of a program. In other words, the boundaries of features are often not the same as the implementation modules in a program. Hence, a long standing challenge faced by the software maintainers is to identify, buried into hundreds of lines of code, relevant feature dependencies while realizing their changes. Existing techniques and tools lack proper modularity support and do not properly inform the boundaries and feature dependencies in the source code. Even after developers spent a huge effort to figure out how to implement their feature changes, they often miss feature dependencies and introduce bugs in their configurable systems.

Over the past two decades an extensive body of literature has emerged to cover a wide range of topics on software engineering for configurable systems. Researchers and practitioners have gathered a good collective understanding of how to design and implement high-quality configurable systems. However, until recently, our knowledge on how to support software developers on maintaining these systems was still very limited. It is stimulating to see a book that makes a significant improvement to modular maintenance of configurable systems. This book is clearly a distinguished asset in the history of software maintenance for product lines and program families.

During the past 5 years, I have had the honor to meet and closely follow the Doctoral research of Márcio Ribeiro, a talented young researcher, who came up with brilliant ideas on how to tame the complexity of maintaining configurable systems. The book characterizes the notion of emergent feature interface, an essential modularity mechanism to support daily tasks of configurable software maintainers. The on-demand computation of emergent feature interfaces is only possible through feature-sensitive data flow analysis, an innovative technique being described in this book. The description and evaluation of emergent feature interfaces are also inspiring, and treated with the rigor that is characteristic of a mature piece of research.

The several awards granted to Márcio's work over the last years are an evidence of the relevance and impact of his research. You should definitely read this book if you want a thorough coverage of an innovative approach that has the potential to shape next-generation tools for maintaining configurable systems.

Rio de Janeiro, December 2013   Alessandro Garcia

Contents

Acronyms

API	Application Programming Interfaces
AST	Abstract Syntax Tree
CFG	Control-Flow Graph
CIDE	Colored IDE
FODA	Feature-Oriented Domain Analysis
SLoC	Source Lines of Code
SPL	Software Product Line
VSoC	Virtual Separation of Concerns

Chapter 1
Introduction

Abstract This chapter introduces the problem that motivates this work and presents a brief overview of this book, explaining why the problem we address is important, how we address this problem, and, finally, how we evaluate the proposed solution.

Keywords Feature dependencies · Software modularity · Software families · Software product lines · Emergent interfaces · Feature-sensitive dataflow analysis

Developers often introduce errors to software systems when they fail to recognize module dependencies [7, 8]. This problem is particularly critical for software families [19], in which features—semantic units by which we differentiate systems [28]—also contain dependencies and can be enabled and disabled at compile time or run time. In this context, features often crosscut each other [17] and share program elements like variables and methods [25]. So, we might have fine-grained code level dependencies crossing feature boundaries, like when a feature assigns a value to a variable read by another feature. In this case, developers can easily miss these dependencies and then, for example, assign a new value to a variable which happens to be correct to the maintained feature, but incorrect to the one that uses this variable. In particular, missing feature dependencies leads to incomplete fixes, which are "introduced by the fact that fixers may forget to fix all the buggy regions with the same root cause" [30].

This feature dependency problem happens since there is no proper feature modularization support. In other words, there is no "mutual agreement between the creator and accessor" [29]. Since this contract does not exist, developers of a feature might actually break another one. Similar issues could also appear when developers assume invalid dependencies, as would be the case if the involved features were mutually exclusive.

In this work, we not only report this feature modularization problem (maintenance in a feature breaks another), but also provide a study with respect to how often it may occur in practice [25]. To do so, we use 43 software families and Software Product Lines (SPLs), where the majority are commonly used in industrial practice.

Also, to solve the code level feature dependency problem, we present in this work the concept of emergent feature modularization [23, 24], which aims to establish contracts between features, to prevent developers from breaking other features when

M. Ribeiro et al., *Emergent Interfaces for Feature Modularization*,
SpringerBriefs in Computer Science, DOI 10.1007/978-3-319-11493-4_1

performing a maintenance task. We call our approach emergent because the interfaces here are neither predefined nor have a rigid structure. Developers do not need to write them. Instead, they emerge on demand to give support for maintenance tasks. To do so, Emergent Interfaces capture dependencies between the feature we are maintaining and the others we might impact with our maintenance, making developers aware of them. This way, Emergent Interfaces provide information to the developer, so she can maintain a feature and keep the other ones safe, being consistent with previous research [30]: "if all such potential 'influenced code' is clearly presented to developers, they may have better chances to detect the errors." Besides, Emergent Interfaces allow us to change a feature abstracting details of the surrounding feature code. Differently from our proposal, traditional interfaces fail to capture fine-grained dependencies and require programming constructs [22].

To better study and understand our proposal, in this work we focus on software families [19] and product lines [10, 11, 21] that implement features with preprocessor directives, which are widely used to implement compile time variability in industrial practice [1, 3, 4, 12, 13, 15, 20]. Also, to aid comprehensibility [18], we consider the support for Virtual Separation of Concerns (VSoC) [13], which allows developers to hide code fragments not related to features associated with a given task. In this manner, we allow developers to focus on a feature and its (emergent) interface without the distraction brought by other features.

Roughly, our technique works as follows: the developer first selects the feature code to maintain. We associate this selection with a feature or a set of features. Then, based on the dependencies, information (like variable usage) with respect to the other features and their combinations emerge through an interface.

To capture the mentioned dependencies, we can rely on dataflow analyses, essential for supporting optimization [2] and maintenance [24] tasks. However, since code assets implemented using preprocessors might not be valid program elements, existing dataflow analyses cannot be directly used to analyze such assets. So, we have to generate all possible method variants and then execute dataflow analyses on each variant separately. However, this approach might range from costly to prohibitive for non-trivial software families and product lines.

To handle this problem and enable more efficient dataflow analysis for preprocessor-based families and product lines, we propose two approaches [5, 6] for taking any standard *intraprocedural* dataflow analysis and automatically lifting it into a corresponding feature-sensitive analysis that we can use to directly analyze code assets. Both approaches analyze all configurations and thus avoid explicitly generating and analyzing all possible method variants. Based on the feature-sensitive analyses results, we generate the Emergent Interfaces. Although we focus on preprocessor-based families and product lines developed with conditional compilation constructs, our results apply for similar annotative variability mechanisms, like background colors [13].

To support developers with Emergent Interfaces, we provide a prototype tool—named Emergo [26, 27]—based on Eclipse plug-ins [9]. Emergo can compute Emergent Interfaces based on feature dependencies between methods or within a single method, by using *interprocedural* or *intraprocedural* feature-sensitive dataflow analysis, respectively.

To evaluate the potential of Emergent Interfaces to reduce maintenance effort, we conduct and report an empirical study that uses proxy metrics [14, 16] such as the *number of features* that developers have to analyze with and without Emergent Interfaces. For example, when changing a variable value, developers should analyze if there are dependencies between the feature they are maintaining and the other ones. Because Emergent Interfaces capture dependencies, they might reduce effort by focusing on the features we might indeed impact. In contrast, without Emergent Interfaces, developers do not have any information about the existence or absence of dependencies. So, they still need to check this in the existing features. We conclude that Emergent Interfaces achieve maintenance effort reduction mainly in methods with many preprocessor directives. To perform this evaluation, we rely on the already mentioned 43 preprocessor-based software families and product lines.

Also, we provide an evaluation with respect to the performance of both feature-sensitive analyses we introduce in this book. Investigating which one is the fastest plays an important role in deciding which one we should use in interactive tools like Emergo. We obtain evidence that the feature-sensitive approach runs faster (when compared to the feature-oblivious approach) on software families and product lines with high feature usage.

We organize the remainder of this book as follows:

- Chapter 2 reviews essential concepts used throughout this book;
- Chapter 3 discusses the feature dependency problem. In particular, we illustrate three scenarios where this problem occurs and provide a study that reveals that it might be quite common in practice;
- Chapter 4 presents our Emergent Interfaces approach. Firstly, we revisit the problematic scenarios of the previous chapter and then we present our approach as follows: the definition; the general idea; the feature-sensitive analyses; how we generate Emergent Interfaces based on these analyses; the tool called Emergo to support developers with Emergent Interfaces; how we improve expressiveness of Emergent Interfaces by using contracts; and, finally, how we can use Emergent Interfaces in other mechanisms apart from preprocessors;
- Chapter 5 details our evaluation with respect to maintenance effort and performance, where we compare our feature-sensitive approaches with the feature-oblivious one;
- Chapter 6 discusses the related work; and
- Chapter 7 presents the final considerations of this book.

This book contains adapted and extended parts of the authors previous work [5, 6, 22–27], and is essentially a major revision of the first author Ph.D. thesis. We list the previous work in what follows, according to the *ACM Author Rights and Publishing Policy, item 2.4*[1]:

---

[1] http://www.acm.org/publications/policies/copyright_policy.

- *Emergent Feature Modularization*, in Proceedings of the International Conference on Object-Oriented Programming Systems Languages and Applications Companion, © ACM, 2010. http://dx.doi.org/10.1145/1869542.1869545
- *Towards Feature Modularization*, in Proceedings of the International Conference on Object-Oriented Programming Systems Languages and Applications Companion, © ACM, 2010. http://dx.doi.org/10.1145/1869542.1869585
- *On the Impact of Feature Dependencies when Maintaining Preprocessor-based Software Product Lines*, in Proceedings of the 10th International Conference on Generative Programming and Component Engineering, © ACM, 2011. http://dx.doi.org/10.1145/2047862.2047868
- *On the Impact of Feature Dependencies when Maintaining Preprocessor-based Software Product Lines*, in ACM SIGPLAN Notices, 47, 3, March 2012 © ACM, 2012. http://dx.doi.org/10.1145/2189751.2047868
- *Intraprocedural Dataflow Analysis for Software Product Lines*, in Proceedings of the 11th International Conference on Aspect-Oriented Software Development, © ACM, 2012. http://dx.doi.org/10.1145/2162049.2162052
- *Emergo: A Tool for Improving Maintainability of Preprocessor-based Product Lines*, in Proceedings of the 11th International Conference on Aspect-Oriented Software Development Companion, © ACM, 2012. http://dx.doi.org/10.1145/2162110.2162128
- *Feature Maintenance with Emergent Interfaces*, in Proceedings of the 36th International Conference on Software Engineering, © ACM, 2014. http://dx.doi.org/10.1145/2568225.2568289

All co-authors are aware of this book publication and now we acknowledge them: Társis Tolêdo, Johnni Winther, Felipe Queiroz, Christian Kästner, Leopoldo Teixeira, Humberto Pacheco, and Sérgio Soares.

References

1. Adams, B., De Meuter, W., Tromp, H., Hassan, A.E.: Can we refactor conditional compilation into aspects? In: Proceedings of the 8th International Conference on Aspect-Oriented Software Development (AOSD), pp. 243–254. ACM (2009)
2. Aho, A., Lam, M., Sethi, R., Ullman, J.: Compilers: Principles, Techniques, and Tools, 2nd edn. Addison-Wesley, Lebanon (2006)
3. Alves, V., Matos P., Jr, Cole, L., Borba, P., Ramalho, G.: Extracting and evolving mobile games product lines. In: Proceedings of the 9th International Software Product Line Conference (SPLC). Lecture Notes in Computer Science, vol. 3714, pp. 70–81. Springer (2005)
4. Anastasopoulos, M., Gacek, C.: Implementing product line variabilities. In: Proceedings of the 2001 Symposium on Software Reusability (SSR), pp. 109–117. ACM Press (2001)
5. Brabrand, C., Ribeiro, M., Tolêdo, T., Borba, P.: Intraprocedural dataflow analysis for software product lines. Lecture Notes in Computer Science: Transactions on Aspect-Oriented Software Development I , pp. 73–108. Springer (2012)
6. Brabrand, C., Ribeiro, M., Tolêdo, T., Winther, J., Borba, P.: Lecture Notes in Computer Science: Transactions on Aspect-Oriented Software Development I. Intraprocedural dataflow analysis for software product lines, pp. 73–108. Springer (2012)

7. Cataldo, M., Herbsleb, J.D.: Factors leading to integration failures in global feature-oriented development: an empirical analysis. In: Proceedings of the 33rd International Conference on Software Engineering (ICSE), pp. 161–170. ACM (2011)

8. Cataldo, M., Mockus, A., Roberts, J.A., Herbsleb, J.D.: Software dependencies, work dependencies, and their impact on failures. IEEE Trans. Softw. Eng. **35**(6), 864–878 (2009)

9. Clayberg, E., Rubel, D.: Eclipse: Building Commercial-Quality Plug-ins. Addison-Wesley Professional (2006)

10. Clements, P., Northrop, L.: Software Product Lines: Practices and Patterns. Addison-Wesley, Boston (2002)

11. van der Linden, F., Schmid, K., Rommes, E.: Software Product Lines in Action: the Best Industrial Practice in Product Line Engineering. Springer, Berlin (2007)

12. Ernst, M.D., Badros, G.J., Notkin, D.: An empirical analysis of c preprocessor use. IEEE Trans. Softw. Eng. **28**, 1146–1170 (2002)

13. Kästner, C., Apel, S., Kuhlemann, M.: Granularity in software product lines. In: Proceedings of the 30th International Conference on Software Engineering (ICSE), pp. 311–320. ACM (2008)

14. Keeney, R.L., Gregory, R.S.: Selecting attributes to measure the achievement of objectives. Oper. Res. **53**(1), 1–11 (2005)

15. Kolb, R., Muthig, D., Patzke, T., Yamauchi, K.: A case study in refactoring a legacy component for reuse in a product line. In: Proceedings of the 21st International Conference on Software Maintenance (ICSM), pp. 369–378. IEEE Computer Society (2005)

16. McKay, S.K., Pruitt, B.A., Harberg, M., Covich, A.P., Kenney, M.A., Fischenich, J.C.: Metric development for environmental benefits analysis. Technical Report ERDC TN-EMRRP-EBA-4 (2010)

17. Liebig, J., Apel, S., Lengauer, C., Kästner, C., Schulze, M.: An analysis of the variability in forty preprocessor-based software product lines. In: Proceedings of the 32nd International Conference on Software Engineering (ICSE), pp. 105–114. ACM (2010)

18. Parnas, D.L.: On the criteria to be used in decomposing systems into modules. CACM **15**(12), 1053–1058 (1972)

19. Parnas, David L.: On the design and development of program families. IEEE Trans. Softw. Eng. **2**(1), 1–9 (1976)

20. Patzke, T., Muthig, D.: Product line implementation technologies. Technical Report 057.02/E, Fraunhofer Institut Experimentelles Software Engineering (2002)

21. Pohl, K., Bockle, G., van der Linden, F.J.: Software Product Line Engineering. Springer, Berlin (2005)

22. Ribeiro, M., Borba, P., Kästner, C.: Feature maintenance with emergent interfaces. In: Proceedings of the International Conference on Software Engineering (ICSE), pp. 989–1000. ACM (2014)

23. Ribeiro, M., Borba, P.: Towards feature modularization. In: Doctoral Symposium of the International Conference on Object-Oriented Programming Systems Languages and Applications (OOPSLA), pp. 225–226. ACM (2010)

24. Ribeiro, M., Pacheco, H., Teixeira, L., Borba, P.: Emergent feature modularization. In: Onward!, Affiliated with the International Conference on Systems, Programming, Languages and Applications: Software for Humanity (SPLASH), pp. 11–18. ACM (2010)

25. Ribeiro, M., Queiroz, F., Borba, P., Tolêdo, T., Brabrand, C., Soares, S.: On the impact of feature dependencies when maintaining preprocessor-based software product lines. In: Proceedings of the 10th International Conference on Generative Programming and Component Engineering (GPCE), pp. 23–32. ACM (2011)

26. Ribeiro, M., Toledo, T., Borba, P., Brabrand, C.: A tool for improving maintainabiliy of preprocessor-based product lines. In: Tools Session of the 2nd Brazilian Congress on Software (CBSoft) (2011)

27. Ribeiro, M., Toledo, T., Winther, J., Brabrand, C., Borba, P.: Emergo: a tool for improving maintainabiliy of preprocessor-based product lines. In: Proceedings of the 11th International Conference on Aspect-Oriented Software Development (AOSD), Companion, Demo Track, pp. 23–26. ACM (2012)

28. Trujillo, S., Batory, D., Diaz, O.: Feature refactoring a multi-representation program into a product line. In: Proceedings of the 5th International Conference on Generative Programming and Component Engineering (GPCE), pp. 191–200. ACM (2006)

29. Wulf, W., Shaw, M.: Global variable considered harmful. SIGPLAN Not. **8**(2), 28–34 (1973)

30. Yin, Z., Yuan, D., Zhou, Y., Pasupathy, S., Bairavasundaram, L.: How do fixes become bugs? In: Proceedings of the 19th ACM SIGSOFT Symposium and the 13th European Conference on Foundations of Software Engineering (ESEC/FSE), pp. 26–36. ACM (2011)

Chapter 2
Software Families, Software Products Lines, and Dataflow Analyses

Abstract In this chapter we review essential concepts we explore in this work. Firstly, we review software families and software product lines, since the problem we address here is critical in these contexts. We show the basic concepts and then move towards conditional compilation with preprocessors, a widely used mechanism to implement features in industrial practice. Despite the widespread usage, conditional compilation has several drawbacks. We then present the Virtual Separation of Concerns (VSoC) approach, which can minimize some of these drawbacks. In this work, we intend to address the lack of feature modularity. Thus, we need to catch dependencies between features and inform developers about them. To do so, we rely on dataflow analyses, the last topic we review in this chapter.

Keywords Sofware families · Software product lines · Preprocessors · Virtual separation of concerns · Modularity · Dataflow analysis · Reaching definitions

2.1 Software Families and Software Product Lines

Software development often relies on version control systems like SVN [19] and CVS [8]. As we implement new functionalities, we put them under version control. In addition, we may remove or modify a functionality that for some reason did not work as expected. In this context, we have one software system per instant of time, as illustrated in Fig. 2.1. Notice that this system contains a base component (*circle*), which is common to all subsequent system versions.

However, having one system per instant is not convenient for large scale software production. For example, if a customer requires a system composed of the *circle*, *square*, and *triangle* components, we are not able to deliver such a product immediately because there is no version in the timeline that contains these three components—*circle*, *square*, and *triangle*—together. What we could do is to find a product that is an approximation of the one we need to build. Taking t3 as an example, we remove the *diamond* and then add the *triangle* component. However, removing and adding components may be a non-trivial task, being error-prone and increasing effort. In particular, *square* and *triangle* might have never worked together, which might increase our test case suite. As can be seen, all these activities may impact on time-to-market.

© The Author(s) 2014
M. Ribeiro et al., *Emergent Interfaces for Feature Modularization*,
SpringerBriefs in Computer Science, DOI 10.1007/978-3-319-11493-4_2

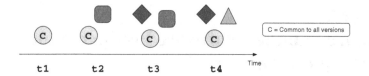

Fig. 2.1 One product per time

To improve this process, instead of having only one system per instant of time, we define a set of systems. This set contains similar systems differentiated by features [7]. We consider this set to constitute a *software family*, since we study the commonalities of the set and then the variabilities of the individual family members [21]. Although these members contain significant differences, it usually pays to learn the common properties of all systems before studying the details of any one [21]. This enables software reuse, for example, being important to deal with customers request more easily.

To enable the systematic construction of these individual systems with mass customization, we need to consider a product line. Basically, every software product line is a software family, but the opposite is not true. We explain product lines in what follows.

A Software Product Line (SPL) is *a set of software-intensive systems that share a common, managed set of features satisfying the specific needs of a particular market segment or mission and that are developed from a common set of core assets in a prescribed way* [7]. In this context, core assets means any artifact used to instantiate more than one product [18]. Notice that these assets are not only code artifacts, but also any element used to develop the final product. This way, requirements, the software architecture, binary files, image files, test cases, sound files, and documentation are examples of potential core assets. Again, instead of having one product per instant of time, we have a set of core assets. Customers choose their particular product configurations, and then we build the product by reusing the core assets, usually bringing significant productivity and time-to-market improvements [7, 17, 22].

SPLs define two processes. The first one comprehends the core assets development. It establishes the reusable platform and consequently the commonalities and variabilities of the SPL, being known as *Domain Engineering*. The second one is responsible for deriving product line applications based on the predefined core assets. Therefore, it ensures the correct binding of the variabilities according to the application-specific needs. Such product development process is known as *Application Engineering*.

Some advantages of adopting the SPL approach are outlined below:

- **Reduction of development costs**: when artifacts are reusable in several different products, this implies a cost reduction for each product, since there is no need to develop such components from scratch. However, there is a cost associated with the beginning of the SPL design. In other words, before building final products, it is necessary firstly to design and implement the core assets so that we can reuse them. This way, before having one single product, we already have an upfront

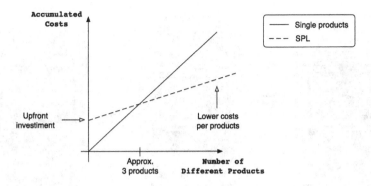

Fig. 2.2 Costs to develop single systems compared to the SPL engineering

investment. Empirical studies reveal that the upfront investments to design a SPL from scratch usually pay-off around three products [7]. Therefore, the accumulated costs are the same when developing three products without the SPL engineering and three products by using the SPL engineering (see Fig. 2.2). However, when the number of products increases, we have lower costs per product with the SPL approach;

- **Enhancement of quality**: the core assets of a SPL are reused in many products. In this way, they are tested and reviewed many times, which means that there is a higher chance of detecting faults and correcting them, which improves the quality of the products;
- **Reduction of time-to-market**: initially, the time-to-market of the SPL is high, because the core assets must be developed first. Afterwards, the time-to-market is reduced, because many previously developed components might be reused for each new product.

However, to gain all of these advantages, managing the SPL features in a suitable way is essential. In this context, features are the semantic units by which different products within a SPL can be differentiated and defined [27], playing a key role for mass customization. Features are also defined as prominent and stakeholder visible aspects, qualities, or characteristics of a software system or systems [10]. The Feature-Oriented Domain Analysis (FODA) approach is a domain analysis that focuses on the description of SPL commonalities and variabilities by means of features.

To illustrate feature examples, we use the *Best Lap* product line.[1] *Best Lap* is a race game where the player tries to achieve the best time in one lap and qualify for the pole position. It has approximately 15KLOC and is highly variant due to portability constraints: it should run on several platforms. In fact, the game is deployed on 65 devices [3]. Figure 2.3 illustrates the race game.

---

[1] *Best lap* is a commercial product developed by Meantime Mobile Creations. http://www.meantime.com.br/.

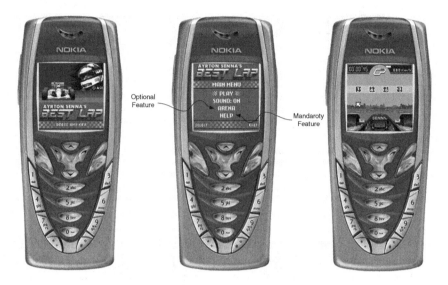

Fig. 2.3 *Help* (mandatory) and *arena* (optional) features in *Best Lap*

In this context, there are functionalities that are common to all *Best Lap* products. For instance, the menu item "Help" is mandatory, which means that all products contain this item. On the other hand, depending on the mobile device, some features are not available. For example, the *arena* feature (see the "Arena" menu item in Fig. 2.3) is an optional feature for publishing the scores obtained by the player on the network. This way, players around the world are able to compare their results. In addition, we may have features not visible for some stakeholders. For example, each device uses an API provided by the mobile manufacturer. Because it is not possible to use two APIs from two different manufacturers in the same product, we say that API is an alternative feature (or mutually exclusive feature).

The FODA approach represents in a compact way all possible products of a SPL by using a so called feature model. Besides describing features, the feature model provides a feature diagram (tree) and defines constraints between features. Figure 2.4 illustrates a small feature model of *Best Lap*. The feature diagram depicts a hierarchical decomposition of features with mandatory (*filled circle*), optional (*open circle*), and alternative (*open arc*) relationships. As can be seen, we have two feature constraints in this feature model. Firstly, *Nokia* and *Motorola* are alternative. Thus, they can never be together in the same product. Secondly, the *arena* feature only works with the *Motorola* API, so *Arena* → *Motorola*.

Conceptually, a feature model is a propositional logic formula [4]. For instance, the above feature model is captured by the formula:

Fig. 2.4 Bestlap feature model

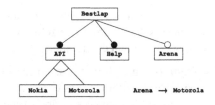

Fig. 2.5 Arena feature implemented with conditional compilation

```
public void computeLevel() {
    ...
    ...
    totalScore = ...;
    ...
    ...
    #ifdef ARENA
    NetworkFacade.setScore(totalScore);
    NetworkFacade.setLevel(this.getCurrentLevel());
    #endif
}
```

$$\psi_{FM} = \texttt{API} \land \texttt{Help} \land (\texttt{Nokia} \leftrightarrow \neg\texttt{Motorola}) \land (\texttt{Arena} \rightarrow \texttt{Motorola})$$

This feature model corresponds to the following set of valid configurations:

$$\llbracket \psi_{FM} \rrbracket = \{\{\texttt{API}, \texttt{Help}, \texttt{Nokia}\},$$
$$\{\texttt{API}, \texttt{Help}, \texttt{Motorola}\},$$
$$\{\texttt{API}, \texttt{Help}, \texttt{Motorola}, \texttt{Arena}\}\}$$

2.1.1 Conditional Compilation

Features are often implemented using mechanisms like preprocessors [2, 11, 15]. Conditional Compilation is a well-known and widely used mechanism for handling variabilities in languages such as C and C++. This mechanism is used at pre-compile time. The preprocessor analyzes the code that should be compiled or not based on directive tags. In this manner, if the directive tag is true, the code must be compiled. Otherwise, the preprocessor ignores such code snippet and it is not compiled.

Conditional compilation directives such as #ifdef and #endif encompass code associated with optional and alternative features, for example. Then, to remove a feature from the final product, we set to false the directive tag correspondent to the feature. Figure 2.5 illustrates a snippet of the *arena* feature implemented using conditional compilation.

Conditional compilation consists of a very simple programming model. There is no need to learn new languages. Besides, conditional compilation addresses not only fine-grained variabilities, but also coarsed-grained ones, like when we encompass an entire class with an #ifdef directive. However, despite their widespread use, preprocessors suffer of several drawbacks, including no support for separation of concerns [9, 12, 25]. In what follows, we provide an overview of some arguments against conditional compilation:

- **Comprehensibility**: we can potentially use many #ifdef directives—that might be nested—within a class or even within a single method. Additionally, the base code (the one without #ifdefs) and feature code may have dependencies which are difficult to locate and understand. For example, the base code may declare a variable and the feature code might use it. Mixing #ifdef directives with the source code complicates the task of understanding and even reading the code. This way, maintaining it is difficult as well. Therefore, maintenance tasks in one particular feature are problematic. Developers cannot focus on such a feature, since the other ones might distract them [12]. Besides, the total source lines of code (SLoC) sometimes increases significantly due to the #ifdef directives;
- **Separation of concerns**: a preprocessor-based implementation scatters feature code across the entire base code, leading to tangling and traceability problems [12]. This way, instead of looking at one single module, we need to search in many code artifacts for snippets of the feature we are maintaining. In addition, feature tangling distracts the developer, as mentioned. Usually, it is difficult to focus on one particular feature;
- **Sensitivity to subtle errors**: when using conditional compilation, developers are prone to introduce subtle errors [12]. For instance, they can annotate an opening bracket but not the closing one. And this situation gets even worse: compilers are not able to detect this syntactic error unless the developer eventually tries to build the system with the problematic variant. One can build all variants to detect problems like these. However, depending on the number of features, this ranges from costly to prohibitive. For example, a small SPL with no feature constraints and 10 optional features that can be arbitrarily combined requires $2^{10} = 1024$ distinct products to be compiled.

Next, we present an approach that aims at reducing these drawbacks.

2.1.2 Virtual Separation of Concerns

Virtual Separation of Concerns (VSoC) [11] allows developers to hide feature code not relevant to the current task, being important to reduce some of the preprocessors drawbacks. Using this approach, developers can, to some extent, maintain a feature without being distracted by the others, aiding comprehensibility. Figure 2.6 shows the *arena* feature hidden.

In this context, #ifdef directives are no longer needed. For feature annotations, developers rely on background colors, so that code fragments belonging to a feature are shown with a background color. For our example, the background color associated with *arena* is gray. VSoC relies on tools for hiding and coloring the feature code. One such tool is the Colored IDE (CIDE) [11].

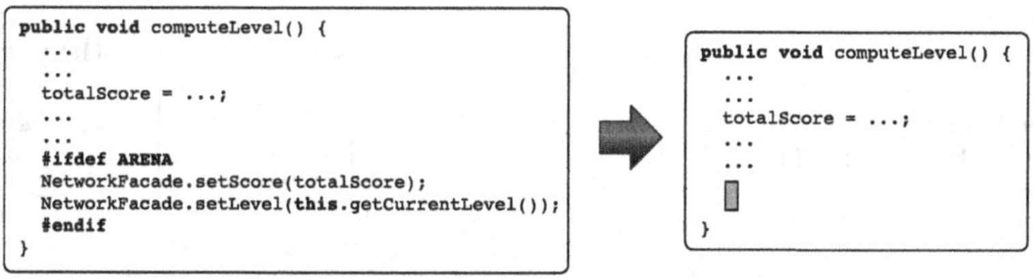

Fig. 2.6 From conditional compilation to VSoC: arena feature hidden

Now, we revisit each problem discussed in Sect. 2.1.1. The idea consists of discussing the conditional compilation drawbacks that VSoC minimizes.

- **Comprehensibility and separation of concerns**: when using the VSoC approach, it is possible to separate concerns by using views. Technically, this is done by hiding the code not related to the feature we are maintaining. The approach is called virtual since the hidden code is still there. This way, VSoC is purely annotative: there is no physical code extraction to other modularization units such as aspects [13]. Besides, when using the VSoC approach, we abandon #ifdef directives, avoiding code pollution and decreasing the system size in terms of SLoC. We employ background colors, instead;

- **Sensitivity to subtle errors**: to avoid problems of wrong annotations, VSoC allows only disciplined feature annotations. To define disciplined annotations, we use the following definition [16]: "annotations on one or a sequence of entire functions are disciplined. Furthermore, annotations on one or a sequence of entire statements are disciplined. All other annotations are undisciplined." So, we can annotate program elements such as entire classes, methods, and statements. However, we cannot annotate, for instance, an if statement and its opening bracket without the closing one. In such a case, the annotation is undisciplined, and the tool does not allow it. Also, we cannot annotate not optional nodes—like the return type of a method—because it would invalidate the AST [11]. This approach limits the expressive power of annotations in exchange for avoiding syntax errors. In addition, CIDE provides a product-line-aware type system. The idea consists of checking if the variants are well-typed. For example, CIDE shows an error when we annotate a variable declaration but not the variable use; or if we annotate the only return statement of a method.

Despite reducing some drawbacks, developers are still not aware of feature dependencies. Next, we present dataflow analysis, the technique we use to capture these dependencies throughout this work.

Fig. 2.7 A simple example
program and its
corresponding control-flow
graph. **a** An example
program. . ., **b** . . .and its CFG

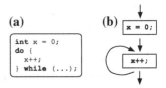

2.2 Dataflow Analysis

In this section, we review dataflow analysis. We present the three constituents of
dataflow analysis (control-flow graph, lattice, and transfer functions) in Sect. 2.2.1.
Then, in Sect. 2.2.2, we show one type of dataflow analysis named reaching definitions.

2.2.1 The Three Constituents

The three constituents of a dataflow analysis [14] are:

- a *control-flow graph* (on which we perform the analysis);
- a *lattice* (representing values of interest during the analysis); and
- *transfer functions* (that simulate the program execution at compile-time).

In what follows, we recall each of these three constituents (Sects. 2.2.1.1, 2.2.1.2,
and 2.2.1.3) and describe how we may combine them to analyze an input program
(Sect. 2.2.1.4) [5, 6].

2.2.1.1 Control-Flow Graph

Conceptually, a control-flow graph (CFG) is the abstraction of an input program on
which a dataflow analysis runs. A CFG is a directed graph where the nodes are the
statements of the input program and the edges represent flow of control according to
the semantics of the programming language. Some analyses use *forward* flow and
others use *backwards* flow. The difference is that we reverse the directions of the
arrows. Figure 2.7a depicts a tiny program fragment and its corresponding control-
flow graph (Fig. 2.7b). We build a control-flow graph inductively from the syntactic
structure of the program, although exceptions and virtual dispatching may complicate
this process. An analysis may be *intraprocedural* or *interprocedural*, depending on
how functions are handled in the CFG.

Fig. 2.8 A Hasse diagram
of a lattice for sign analysis

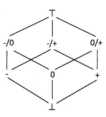

2.2.1.2 Lattice

In dataflow analysis, we carefully arrange the information calculated by the analysis in a lattice, $\mathscr{L} = (D, \sqsubseteq)$ where D is a set of elements and $\sqsubseteq$ is a *partial-order* on the elements.

Lattices are usually and conveniently described diagrammatically using so-called *Hasse Diagrams* as in Fig. 2.8, which depicts a lattice for analysing the sign of an integer. Each element of the lattice captures information of interest by the analysis we are executing. For example, "+" represents the fact that the value is always positive, "0 / -" that the value is always either zero-or-negative. Moreover, a lattice often has two special elements; $\bot$ at the bottom of the lattice which usually means "not analyzed yet" whereas $\top$ at the top of the lattice usually means "we don't know" the value at compile-time.

The partial ordering of the elements is depicted using the convention that $x \sqsubseteq y$ if and only if x is depicted below y in the diagram (according to the lines of the diagram). For example, $\bot \sqsubseteq +$ (since $\bot$ is directly below +) and $0 \sqsubseteq \top$ (since 0 is transitively below $\top$), whereas $- \not\sqsubseteq 0$ and $- \not\sqsubseteq 0/+$.

In this context, the order is important during analysis as it induces a *least upper bound* operator, $\sqcup$, on the lattice elements which we use to combine information in the analysis when control-flows meet. For instance, $\bot \sqcup 0 = 0$, $0 \sqcup + = 0/+$, and $- \sqcup 0/+ = \top$.

Notice that the lattice we present arranges signs of an integer. However, the information the lattice should deal with depends on the analysis we intend to perform. For instance, if we need to analyze the value of a variable, the lattice would arrange assignments to that variable. To better explain, consider the left-hand side of Fig. 2.9, which illustrates another toy program containing assignments to the variable x. The right-hand side presents the lattice. Not surprisingly, x = 0 and x = 9 indicate that x is assigned to 0 and 9, respectively.

As explained, $\top$ represents the fact that "we don't know" the value of x at compile time. Therefore, x is assigned to either 0 or 9. This situation happens right before the call to method m, exactly where the control-flows meet. During the analysis, we combine information by using the least upper bound operator: $\{x = 0\} \sqcup \{x = 9\} = \top$.

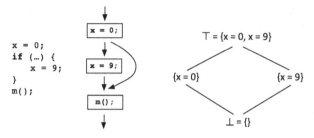

Fig. 2.9 Lattice arranging variable assignments

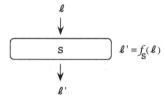

Fig. 2.10 Illustration of the effect of transfer function, f_S

$$f_{x=0}(\ell) = 0 \qquad\qquad f_{x++}(\ell) = \begin{cases} \top & \ell \in \{-/+, -/0, \top\} \\ + & \ell \in \{0, +, 0/+\} \\ -/0 & \ell = - \\ \bot & \ell = \bot \end{cases}$$

Fig. 2.11 Transfer functions for x = 0 and x++

2.2.1.3 Transfer Functions

In a dataflow analysis, each statement, S, of the program has an associated transfer function, $f_S : D \to D$, which simulates execution of S at compile-time (with respect to what is being analyzed). Figure 2.10 illustrates the effect of executing transfer function f_S; lattice element, ℓ, flows into the statement node, the transfer function computes $\ell' = f_S(\ell)$, and the result, ℓ', flows out of the node.

As an example, Fig. 2.11 illustrates transfer functions for two assignment statements. We use these functions for analyzing the sign of variable x using the sign lattice in Fig. 2.8

Now, we detail each function. The first one, $f_{x=0}$, is the constant zero function capturing the fact that x will always have the value zero after executing x = 0. The transfer function, f_{x++}, simulates the execution of x++; e.g., if x was negative ($\ell = -$) prior to execution, we know that its value after execution will always be negative-or-zero ($\ell' = -/0$).

Analogously, we have transfer functions when dealing with other type of information [26], like when the lattice arranges variable assignments. For example, the transfer function $f_{x=9}$ simulates the execution of the x = 9 statement.

Fig. 2.12 Applying the
transfer function for
the x = 9 statement

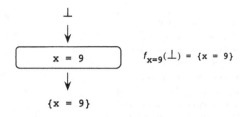

Figure 2.12 depicts that before executing the assignment, we do not know the value of x. Then, the $\bot$ element flows into the statement and we execute function $f_{x=9}(\bot) = \{x = 9\}$. It is easy to notice that now we know the value of x, i.e., x = 9.

Depending on the analysis, the transfer function that deals with assignments is a bit more complicated, as we shall see in Sect. 2.2.2, where we illustrate the transfer function for the reaching definition analysis.

2.2.1.4 Analyzing a Program

Figure 2.13 illustrates how we combine the three constituents to perform dataflow analysis of the input program from Fig. 2.7a. In this context, we first build a control-flow graph (Fig. 2.7b) and annotate with program points which are the *entry* and *exit* points of the statement nodes of the CFG (depicted as gray circles in Fig. 2.13a). In our example, there are four points labelled with the letters a to d. Second, we turn the annotated CFG into a *whole-program transfer function*, $T : D^4 \rightarrow D^4$, which works on four copies of the lattice, $\mathcal{L}$, since we have four program points (a to d). The entry point, a, is assigned an initialization value which depends on the analysis (for the sign analysis it is bottom, $a = \bot$). For each of the program points, we capture the effect of the program using the statement transfer functions for simulating the effect of statements (e.g., $b = f_{x=0}(a)$). Also, we use the least-upper bound operator to combine flows (for instance, $c = b \sqcup d$). For our tiny program, the whole-program transfer function becomes:

$$T((a, b, c, d)) = (\bot, f_{x\,=\,0}(a), b \sqcup d, f_{x++}(c))$$

Then, we use the Fixed-Point Theorem [20] to compute the fixed-point of the function, T, by computing $T^i(\bot)$ for increasing values of i (see the columns of Fig. 2.13c), until nothing changes.

Figure 2.13c shows that we reach the fixed-point in five iterations (see $T^4(\bot) = T^5(\bot)$). Therefore, the result of the analysis is:

$$T((\bot, 0, 0/+, +)) = (\bot, 0, 0/+, +)$$

Fig. 2.13 An input program is turned into a CFG annotated with program points (here, a, b, c, and d); which gives rise to a whole-program transfer function, $T : D^4 \to D^4$; for which we compute the least fixed point by computing $T^i(\bot)$ for increasing i, until nothing changes. **a** CFG. **b** Whole-program transfer function, T. **c** Fixed-point iteration

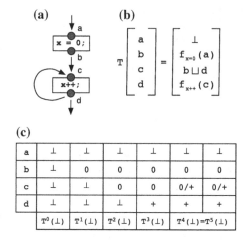

(a)   (b)

(c)

a	$\bot$	$\bot$	$\bot$	$\bot$	$\bot$	$\bot$
b	$\bot$	0	0	0	0	0
c	$\bot$	$\bot$	0	0	0/+	0/+
d	$\bot$	$\bot$	$\bot$	+	+	+
	$T^0(\bot)$	$T^1(\bot)$	$T^2(\bot)$	$T^3(\bot)$	$T^4(\bot)$=$T^5(\bot)$	

This means that "$a =\bot$, $b = 0$, $c = 0/+$, $d = +$" is the unique least fixed-point of T. So, we can deduce that the value of the variable x is always zero at program point b, it is zero-or-positive at point c, and positive at point d.

2.2.2 Reaching Definitions

In this section we present a common dataflow analysis named reaching definitions. The analysis idea consists of determining statically which variable definitions can reach a given program point p. In this context, every assignment to a variable x is a definition. This way, a definition d reaches a point p if there exists a path from the point immediately following d to p such that d is not killed (redefined) along that path [1]. We kill the definition of x if there exists any other assignment to x in another point along the path.

We summarize these concepts by using an example. Figure 2.14a shows a definition in the beginning of the program: tS = p. As Fig. 2.14b depicts, this definition does not reach point 6, since we kill tS = p in all paths from the definition to this point. tS = x kills tS = p in path $1 \to 2 \to 3 \to 5 \to 6$. Analogously, tS = y kills tS = p in path $1 \to 2 \to 4 \to 5 \to 6$. On the other hand, the definition tS = y reaches point 6 in path $4 \to 5 \to 6$. No definition in this path kills tS = y.

Reaching definitions are used to compute *use-def* and *def-use* graphs. The def-use graph is similar to a CFG, except that edges go from definitions to possible uses [23]. The use-def is similar but goes in the opposite way. Figure 2.14c depicts the def-use graph of our small program. These graphs are the basis for compiler optimizations, such as dead code elimination, code motion, and constant propagation [23].

When using reaching definitions, we compute analysis information with respect to assignments. This way, we store them in the lattice. Now, we discuss the transfer

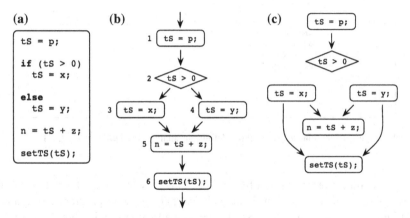

Fig. 2.14 According to the reaching definitions analysis, tS = p does not reach point 6; reaching definitions are also useful to generate def-use graphs. **a** Program. **b** CFG. **c** Def-use graph

functions for reaching definitions. In this context, when executing the following statement, where d means definition,

$$d : tS = x;$$

we "generate" the definition of variable tS. At the same time, we "kill" the other definitions of this variable. This way, we might express our transfer function, f_d, as:

$$f_d(in) = gen_d \cup (in - kill_d)$$

where gen_d is the set of definitions generated by d; $kill_d$ is the set of definitions that d kills; and in is the set of definitions that flows into the definition d we are analyzing. Taking the following program as an example

$$d_1 : x = 1;$$
$$d_2 : y = 2;$$
$$d_3 : x = 2;$$
$$d_4 : a = x + y;$$

and applying the transfer function for definition d_3, we have:

$$f_{d_3}(in) = gen_{d_3} \cup (in - kill_{d_3})$$
$$f_{d_3}(in) = \{x = 2\} \cup (\{x = 1, y = 2\} - \{x = 1\})$$
$$f_{d_3}(in) = \{x = 2\} \cup \{y = 2\}$$
$$f_{d_3}(in) = \{x = 2, y = 2\}$$

Therefore, the assignment x = 1 does not reach the point after d_3, since we killed it due to x = 2.

```
protected void flowThrough(FlowSet source, Unit unit, FlowSet dest) {
  if (unit instanceof AssignStmt) {
    AssignStmt assignment = (AssignStmt) unit;
    kill(source, assignment, dest);
    gen(dest, assignment);
  } else {
    source.copy(dest);
  }
}
```

Fig. 2.15 Transfer function for the reaching definitions analysis implemented in SOOT

To better illustrate this transfer function, we now present an implementation based on SOOT [24], an optimization framework for analyzing Java programs. To implement intraprocedural analyses in SOOT, we typically extend either the Forward-FlowAnalysis or the BackwardFlowAnalysis classes. Because the reaching definitions analysis uses the forward flow, we extend the former class. Then, we implement some template methods such as merge (the least upper bound operator), copy (responsible for copying lattice elements), and flowThrough, which represents the transfer function. Figure 2.15 illustrates the flowThrough method.

Notice that this method takes an Unit object as argument, representing the statement in which the transfer function will take place [26]. Also, it has two more arguments: source and dest. The first one is the lattice flowing into the transfer function. In case the statement we are applying the function is an assignment (in SOOT, an instance of the AssignStmt class), we update the lattice accordingly into the dest object by using the gen and kill functions. Otherwise, there is nothing to do. We simply copy the source lattice into the dest (see the else statement in Fig. 2.15).

References

1. Aho, A., Lam, M., Sethi, R., Ullman, J.: Compilers: Principles, Techniques, and Tools, 2nd edn. Addison-Wesley, Boston (2006)
2. Alves, V., Matos P. Jr., Cole, L., Borba, P., Ramalho, G.: Extracting and Evolving Mobile Games Product Lines. In: Proceedings of the 9th International Software Product Line Conference (SPLC), Lecture Notes in Computer Science, vol. 3714, pp. 70–81. Springer (2005)
3. Alves, V.: Implementing Software Product Line Adoption Strategies. Ph.D. thesis, Federal University of Pernambuco (2007)
4. Batory, D.: Feature models, grammars, and propositional formulas. In: Proceedings of the 9th International Conference on Software Product Lines (SPLC), pp. 7–20. Springer, New York (2005)
5. Brabrand, C., Ribeiro, M., Tolêdo, T., Borba, P.: Intraprocedural dataflow analysis for software product lines. In: Proceedings of the 11th International Conference on Aspect-Oriented Software Development (AOSD), pp. 13–24. ACM (2012)
6. Brabrand, C., Ribeiro, M., Tolêdo, T., Winther, J., Borba, P.: Intraprocedural dataflow analysis for software product lines. Lecture Notes in Computer Science: Transactions on Aspect-Oriented Software Development I, pp. 73–108. Springer (2012)

7. Clements, P., Northrop, L.: Software Product Lines: Practices and Patterns. Addison-Wesley, Boston (2002)
8. Concurrent Versions System. http://savannah.nongnu.org/projects/cvs/ (2011)
9. Ernst, M.D., Badros, G.J., Notkin, D.: An empirical analysis of c preprocessor use. IEEE Trans. Softw. Eng. **28**, 1146–1170 (2002)
10. Kang, K.-C., Cohen, S.G., Hess, J.A., Novak, W.E., Spencer Peterson, A.: Feature-Oriented Domain Analysis (FODA). Feasibility Study. Technical Report CMU/SEI-90-TR-21. Software Engineering Institute (1990)
11. Kästner, C., Apel, S., Kuhlemann, M.: Granularity in software product lines. In: Proceedings of the 30th International Conference on Software Engineering (ICSE), pp. 311–320. ACM (2008)
12. Kästner, C., Apel, S.: Virtual separation of concerns—a second chance for preprocessors. J. Object Technol. **8**(6), 59–78 (2009)
13. Kiczales, G., Lamping, J., Mendhekar, A., Maeda, C., Lopes, C., Loingtier, J.-M., Irwin, J.: Aspect-oriented programming. In: Proceedings of European Conference on Object-Oriented Programming (ECOOP). Lecture Notes in Computer Science, pp. 220–242 (1997)
14. Kildall, G.A.: A unified approach to global program optimization. In: Proceedings of the 1st Annual ACM SIGACT-SIGPLAN Symposium on Principles of Programming Languages (POPL), pp. 194–206. ACM (1973)
15. Kolb, R., Muthig, D., Patzke, T., Yamauchi, K.: A case study in refactoring a legacy component for reuse in a product line. In: Proceedings of the 21st International Conference on Software Maintenance (ICSM), pp. 369–378. IEEE Computer Society (2005)
16. Liebig, J., Kästner, C., Apel, S.: Analyzing the discipline of preprocessor annotations in 30 million lines of c code. In: Proceeding of the 10th International Conference on Aspect-Oriented Software Development (AOSD), pp. 191–202. ACM (2011)
17. van der Linden, F., Schmid, K., Rommes, E.: Software Product Lines in Action: The Best Industrial Practice in Product Line Engineering. Springer, Berlin (2007)
18. Matos P. Jr.: Analyzing techniques for implementing product line variabilities. Master's thesis, Federal University of Pernambuco (2008)
19. Pilato, C.M., Collins-Sussman, B., Fitzpatrick, B.W.: Version Control with Subversion, 1st edn. O'Reilly, Sebastopol (2004)
20. Nielson, F., Nielson, H.R., Hankin, C.: Principles of Program Analysis. Springer, New York (1999)
21. Parnas, D.L.: On the design and development of program families. IEEE Trans. Softw. Eng. **2**(1), 1–9 (1976)
22. Pohl, K., Bockle, G., van der Linden, F.J.: Software Product Line Engineering. Springer, Berlin (2005)
23. Schwartzbach, M.I.: Lecture Notes on Static Analysis (2008)
24. Soot: A Java Optimization Framework. http://www.sable.mcgill.ca/soot/ (2010)
25. Spencer, H., Collyer, G.: #ifdef considered harmful, or portability experience with C news. In: Proceedings of the Usenix Summer Technical Conference, pp. 185–198. Usenix Association (1992)
26. Társis Tolêdo.: Dataflow analysis for software product lines. Master's thesis, Federal University of Pernambuco (2013)
27. Trujillo, S., Batory, D., Diaz, O.: Feature refactoring a multi-representation program into a product line. In: Proceedings of the 5th International Conference on Generative Programming and Component Engineering (GPCE), pp. 191–200. ACM (2006)

Chapter 3
Feature Dependencies

Abstract This chapter illustrates feature dependencies. Besides showing scenarios where feature dependencies may lead to problems during maintenance (e.g., a maintenance in one feature breaks the behavior of other features), we assess to what extent these problems may occur in practice. To do so, we count the number of feature dependencies in 43 preprocessor-based real families and product lines.

Keywords Feature dependencies · Preprocessors · Software families · Software product lines · Software maintenance

To better explain the issues due to the lack of feature modularity, in this chapter we outline three concrete scenarios. Although we could illustrate these issues in different contexts, we choose a critical one: software families and product lines, where code fragments are configurable and may not be included in all product configurations. As a result, by selecting valid feature combinations, we can generate many different products. For example, industrial product lines can easily have hundreds of features with a large number of possible derivable products. When maintaining them, the developer must be sure not to break any of the possible products. Furthermore, code level feature dependencies may cross feature boundaries, so that a variable changed in one feature is read by another feature. If developers miss feature dependencies, they might maintain a feature and actually break another one. This happens because there is no "mutual agreement between the creator and accessor" [6], where the *creator* is the feature declaring the variable and the *accessor* is the feature using it. Since this contract does not exist, the feature modularization problem arises.

The problem we outline is shared by implementation approaches that support some form of crosscutting. For example, if we use aspects (or similar techniques) to implement crosscutting features [1], we need to consider potential dependencies between (optional) aspects and classes. In industrial practice, a more common scenario, and the one we focus here, is to use conditional compilation with preprocessor directives, where optional code fragments are merely annotated in base code [3]. Also in this context, dependencies cross method and feature boundaries and may only occur in specific configurations.

To emulate some form of modularity by aiding comprehensibility [4], the scenarios we show in Sect. 3.1 use Virtual Separation of Concerns (VSoC) [2]. Never-

© The Author(s) 2014

M. Ribeiro et al., *Emergent Interfaces for Feature Modularization*,

SpringerBriefs in Computer Science, DOI 10.1007/978-3-319-11493-4_3

theless, notice again that the feature modularity problem we focus here may happen regardless of VSoC or even of the mechanism one employs to implement features. Then, in Sect. 3.2 we bring more evidence that these scenarios can take place when maintaining software families and product lines in practice.

3.1 Maintaining Features

When maintaining features, developers may introduce problems, leading not only to compilation errors, but also behavioral ones. The following scenarios cover these kinds of errors:

- **Scenario 1**: Maintenance in a feature is accomplished only for some products;
- **Scenario 2**: Maintenance in a feature breaks the compilation of another;
- **Scenario 3**: Maintenance in a feature breaks the behavior of another.

3.1.1 Scenario 1: Maintenance in a Feature Is Accomplished only for Some Products

The first scenario comes from *Best Lap*, detailed in Sect. 2.1. In this game, there is a method (`computeLevel`) responsible for computing the game score, as illustrated in Fig. 3.1. The method contains a small rectangle at the end, representing a hidden feature that the developer is neither seeing nor concerned about.

The hidden feature—named *arena*—is an optional feature responsible for publishing the scores obtained by the player on the network. Thus, players around the world are able to compare their results. Notice that the method also contains a variable responsible for storing the player's total score (see `totalScore` in Fig. 3.1).

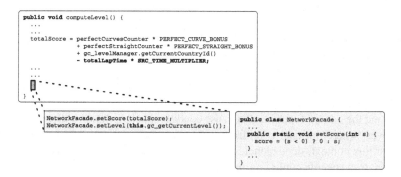

Fig. 3.1 Maintenance correctly accomplished only for products without *arena*

Now, to add penalties in case the player often crashes the car, the developer is supposed to implement the following new requirement in the base code feature: let the game score be not only positive, but also negative.

In order to accomplish the task, a developer would typically look for uses of the `totalScore` variable. If she does not carefully look across feature boundaries (potentially regarding physically separated aspects or code fragments hidden—or not—as part of virtual separation of concerns), considering also feature constraints, she can introduce an error. In this case, she could localize the *maintenance points* (here, the `totalScore` assignment) and change only its value (see the bold line in Fig. 3.1). Building a product with the *arena* feature enabled and running it makes the developer think that everything is correct, since the negative total score appears after the race. But when publishing the score on the network, she notices that the negative score is actually stored as zero (see the expanded *arena* feature code). So, we can conclude that the maintenance was correctly accomplished only for products without *arena*.

Because there are feature dependencies, the developer might be unaware that another feature she is not maintaining uses `totalScore` and should also be changed to correctly complete the maintenance task. In fact, the impact on other features leads to two kinds of problems. The first one is the **Error Introduction**. Here, we can only detect errors when we eventually build and execute a product with the problematic feature combination (with *arena* enabled). Second, searching for feature dependencies (uses of `totalScore`) might increase developers **Effort**. Depending on the number of features, the developer should analyze many of them just to be sure that the change does not impact these features negatively. However, it is possible that some—or even all—features might not need any analysis if they do not use the variables that were changed. Moreover, some features are mutually exclusive, so the presence of feature A prohibits the presence of feature B. In this case, if we are maintaining feature A, there is no need to analyze feature B. Nevertheless, because feature constraints like this might not be explicit in code, developers can assume invalid dependencies and analyze unnecessary code, increasing their maintenance **Effort**.

3.1.2 Scenario 2: Maintenance in a Feature Breaks the Compilation of Another

In practice, developers report warnings raised by unused variables. In particular, they use bug reports to report the problem as well as to propose patches to fix it. This kind of problem is common when considering features, as reported in several bug reports. For example, the left-hand side of Fig. 3.2a, b illustrates two unused variables from the *gnome* bug report system: i[1] and `*env`.[2] They are unused when

---

[1] https://bugzilla.gnome.org/show_bug.cgi?id=167715.

[2] https://bugzilla.gnome.org/show_bug.cgi?id=461011.

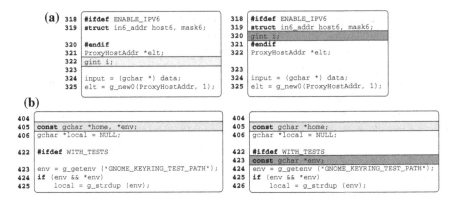

(a)

```
318  #ifdef ENABLE_IPV6              318  #ifdef ENABLE_IPV6
319  struct in6_addr host6, mask6;   319  struct in6_addr host6, mask6;
                                     320  gint i;
320  #endif                          321  #endif
321  ProxyHostAddr *elt;             322  ProxyHostAddr *elt;
322  gint i;
323                                  323
324  input = (gchar *) data;         324  input = (gchar *) data;
325  elt = g_new0(ProxyHostAddr, 1); 325  elt = g_new0(ProxyHostAddr, 1);
```

(b)

```
404                                  404
405  const gchar *home, *env;        405  const gchar *home;
406  gchar *local = NULL;            406  gchar *local = NULL;

422  #ifdef WITH_TESTS               422  #ifdef WITH_TESTS
                                     423  const gchar *env;
423  env = g_getenv ("GNOME_KEYRING_TEST_PATH");   424  env = g_getenv ("GNOME_KEYRING_TEST_PATH");
424  if (env && *env)                425  if (env && *env)
425      local = g_strdup (env);     426      local = g_strdup (env);
```

Fig. 3.2 Diffs illustrating developers moving the declarations into #ifdef statements. **a** Fixing the i unused variable. **b** Fixing the *env unused variable

Fig. 3.3 Breaking feature compilation

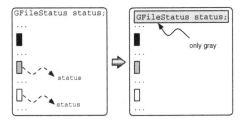

ENABLE_IPV6 and *WITH_TESTS* are not defined, respectively. To fix the problem, developers moved their declaration into #ifdef statements (see the right-hand side in both figures).

Despite simple, notice that fixing unused variables when considering features may lead developers to introduce other problems. To illustrate this, we now describe an example based on a bug report from the *glibc*[3] project. Developers reported that a variable in the mandatory code—named status—was unused. As the left-hand side of Fig. 3.3 depicts, two optional features use the status variable: *gray* and *white*. The problem happens when we compile the product line without either of the features. Without them, the variable is not used anywhere else in the program.

To solve the bug, the developer encompassed the variable declaration with an #ifdef statement (in our case, a color) of the feature that uses such a variable. However, for some reason, she considered only one feature instead of two. In other words, she painted the declaration with only *gray* instead of *gray* and *white* (see the right-hand side of Fig. 3.3).

In fact, she solved the unused variable problem but at the same time introduced a worse problem: now there is an undeclared variable. Indeed, if we build a product without feature *gray*, we remove the variable declaration. Since feature *white* uses it, the code does not compile for products that contain such a feature.

---

[3] http://www.gnu.org/s/libc/.

Because we can still compile products without the *white* feature, developers may not notice the problem. So we have an **Error Introduction**. Further, due to many lines of code and features, the developer probably was confused, forgot—or even did not analyze—the *white* feature. Again, searching for feature dependencies increases **Effort**.

3.1.3 Scenario 3: Maintenance in a Feature Breaks the Behavior of Another

We now present an example based on the *TaRGeT*[4] product line. By using *TaRGeT*, we can automatically generate test cases from use cases specifications. So, we have a form in which users can edit use cases. In this context, developers reported a bug at the editing use case screen: the system shows unconditionally an error message in the use case form (see the top of Fig. 3.4). So, a developer is responsible for fixing this problem. In addition, she should implement the following new requirement: the system should point out which field of the use-case form the user needs to fill again due to validation errors. The idea is to paint the problematic field (in red, for instance) to alert the user she should correct it.

To fix this bug, an `if` statement is enough. To implement the new requirement, she changed the type of the `error` variable from `String` to `String[]`, as illustrated

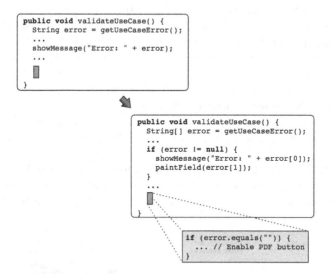

Fig. 3.4 *PDF* feature does not work anymore

---

[4] We do not use *TaRGeT* in our evaluation because very few features use preprocessors. The majority of the features are implemented with components and aspects.

at the bottom of Fig. 3.4. In this manner, she can use the array to store both the error message and the problematic name field.

However, in the same method she is changing there is an optional feature responsible for generating the *PDF* of the use case in case of no error. From the GUI perspective, this feature consists of a small button at the top of the edit use case screen. The developer is unaware of this feature. So, she did not notice that the maintenance introduced a problem in the *PDF* feature: now, because variable error is an array, it will never be equal to the empty string, which means that the *PDF* button will never be enabled (see the *PDF* feature code expanded in Fig. 3.4). Now, PDFs can no longer be generated. Again, both problems—**Error Introduction** and **Effort**—we discussed appear.

3.2 Problem's Dimension

The scenarios discussed so far are susceptible to occur when features *share* elements (i.e., variables, methods). In this work, whenever we have this sharing, we say that there is a *feature dependency* between the involved features. For instance, a mandatory feature may declare a variable and an optional feature might use it (see status and error in Figs. 3.3 and 3.4, respectively).

To assess how often these dependencies occur in practice, we analyze 43 preprocessor-based software families and product lines implemented in C and Java [5]. We built a script tool—based on a recent work [3]—to compute some metrics such as number of methods with preprocessor directives (*MDi*) and number of methods with feature dependencies (*MDe*). In this study we compute the feature dependencies we illustrate in Fig. 3.5. Each rectangle corresponds to a feature. In addition, the alternative features typically correspond to an #ifdef followed by an #else preprocessor directive. However, although we do not show in Fig. 3.5, our script also considers the following directives: #if, #elif, #elifdef, #ifndef, and #elifndef. We represent feature nesting by putting one rectangle inside another. Each ⌐x⌐ represents any use—inside if conditions, general expressions, method actual parameters etc—of the x variable.

We detail the results in Table 3.1. According to them, *MDi* and *MDe* vary significantly across the families and product lines. Some have few directives in their methods. For instance, only 2 % of *irssi* methods have directives. On the other hand,

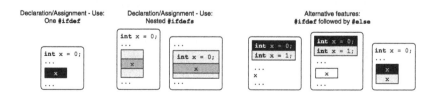

Fig. 3.5 Feature dependencies we consider in our study

Table 3.1 Results on how often feature dependencies occur in practice

Family/SPL	Version	Domain	Language	MDe(%)	MDi(%)	MDe/MDi(%)	NoM	SLoC
berkeley db	5.1.19	Database system	C	7.66	9.07	84.46	10,636	381,315
cherokee	1.0.8	Webserver	C	6.37	8.91	71.52	1,773	52,776
clamav	0.96.4	Antivirus program	C	7	9.35	74.92	3,284	139,054
dia	0.97.1	Diagramming software	C	1.94	3.04	63.75	5,262	137,937
emacs	23.2	Text editor	C	2.45	5.59	43.8	4,333	232,728
freebsd	8.1.0	Operating system	C	6.57	8.98	73.2	130,307	5,694,620
gcc	4.5.1	Compiler framework	C	4.55	5.95	76.4	50,777	1,746,963
ghost script	9.0	Postscript interpreter	C	5.76	7.25	79.44	17,648	677,020
gimp	2.6.11	Graphics editor	C	1.85	2.87	64.48	16,992	596,081
glibc	2.12.1	Programming library	C	5.38	10.03	53.67	7,748	595,525
gnumeric	1.10.11	Spreadsheet application	C	2.24	4.91	45.56	8,711	244,968
gnuplot	4.4.2	Plotting tool	C	10.14	15.41	65.83	1,804	72,556
httpd (apache)	2.2.17	Webserver	C	9.34	12.19	76.59	4,379	214,000
irssi	0.8.15	IRC client	C	1.44	2	71.93	2,843	49,085
linux (kernel)	2.6.36	Operating system	C	3.68	4.9	75.09	208,047	7,121,949
libxml2	2.7.7	XML library	C	22.9	26.92	85.07	5,324	188,960
lighttpd	1.4.28	Webserver	C	11.79	16.73	70.5	831	37,953
lynx	2.8.7	Web browser	C	15.03	21.41	70.18	2,349	111,478
minix	3.1.1	Operating system	C	2.99	4.53	65.96	3,114	113,768
mplayer	1.0rc2	Media player	C	8.82	12	73.51	11,730	475,160
mpsolve	2.2	Mathematical software	C	0.97	1.7	57.14	411	9,562
openldap	2.4.23	LDAP directory service	C	9.91	12.82	77.33	4,026	223,409
openvpn	2.1.3	Security application	C	14.7	17.95	81.91	1,694	48,850
parrot	2.9.1	Virtual machine	C	1.38	6.12	22.52	1,813	104,322

(continued)

Table 3.1 (continued)

Family/SPL	Version	Domain	Language	MDe(%)	MDi(%)	MDe/MDi(%)	NoM	SLoC
php	5.3.3	Program interpreter	C	8.89	11.78	75.51	10,436	664,683
pidgin	2.7.5	Instant messenger	C	3.38	5.26	64.3	10,965	292,311
postgresql	8.4.5	Database system	C	4.5	6.33	71.14	13,199	564,961
privoxy	3.0.16	Proxy server	C	17.84	20.95	85.15	482	26,222
python	2.7	Program interpreter	C	5	27.59	18.14	12,590	362,071
sendmail	8.14.4	Mail transfer agent	C	0.84	4.52	18.52	1,195	85,600
sqlite	3.7.3	Database system	C	9.06	10.64	85.19	3,807	104,594
subversion	1.6.13	Revision control system	C	2.66	4.03	65.99	4,894	558,746
sylpheed	3.0.3	e-mail client	C	5.15	7.57	68	3,634	102,983
tcl	8.5.9	Program interpreter	C	8.4	10.65	78.91	2,761	123,778
vim	7.3	Text editor	C	5.76	11.05	52.14	6,354	274,858
xfig	3.2.5b	Vector graphics editor	C	2.37	3.93	60.24	2,112	71,740
xinelib	1.1.19	Media library	C	6.91	9.88	70.01	10,501	383,727
xorgserver	1.7.1	X server	C	7.39	10.15	72.76	11,425	356,300
xterm	2.6.1	Terminal emulator	C	20.46	24.63	83.08	1,080	49,752
best lap	1.0	Mobile game	Java	11.95	20.7	57.75	343	7,340
juggling	1.0	Mobile game	Java	11.14	16.71	66.67	413	8,279
lampiro	10.4.1	Mobile instant messenger	Java	0.33	2.6	12.5	1,538	31,774
mobile media	0.9	Mobile application	Java	5.8	7.97	72.73	276	5,305
mobile-rss	1.11.1	Mobile feed application	Java	23.84	27.05	88.11	902	27,879

MDi Methods with directives; *MDe* Methods with dependencies; *NoM* Number of methods; *SLoC* Source lines of code. We do not round the numbers to avoid cases where *MDe* = 0%

this number is much bigger in other ones, like *python* (27.59%) and *mobile-rss* (27.05%). Following the convention *average ± standard deviation*, our data reveal that 11.26 ± 7.13% of the methods use preprocessors.

Regarding dependencies, notice that the *MDe* metric is low in many families and product lines. However, we compute this metric with respect to all methods. Rather, if we take only methods with directives into account, we can conclude that, when maintaining features—in other words, when maintaining code with preprocessor directives—the probability of finding dependencies increases a lot. Taking *gnumeric* as an example, only 4.91% of its methods have directives and 2.24% have feature dependencies. Therefore, almost half of methods with directives (45.56%) have feature dependencies (see column *MDe/MDi* in Table 3.1). Our results reveal that

65.92 ± 18.54 % of the methods with directives have dependencies. Thus, the feature dependencies our script considers are indeed common in the families and product lines we analyze.

Nevertheless, it is important to note that our script tool computes only *simple dependencies*, as illustrated in Fig. 3.6a. However, there are more complicated dependencies neglected by our tool, such as *chain of assignments* (Fig. 3.6b) and *interprocedural* (Fig. 3.6c). In the first one, we have a chain because if we change the *aper_size* value, its new value contributes to define the *iommu_size* value which, in its turn, defines the value of *iommu_pages*. And we use this variable in another feature. Besides, our tool does not consider *interprocedural* dependencies, as illustrated in Fig. 3.6c. In this case, we pass a variable as a method parameter and we use it in another feature in the target method.

We do not count neither these two kinds of dependencies nor dependencies such as global variable definition/use and method definition/use. Since all these kinds of dependencies are not present in our statistics, we believe that the real number of feature dependencies susceptible to occur in preprocessor-based software families and product lines is higher.

Another problem with this study is that we do not take the possible feature constraints (from a feature model, for example) into account, which might slightly change the *MDe* results.

Last but not least, we present some dependencies per method of the *berkeley db* software family (see Table 3.2). We choose this family and their methods randomly. Here we only intend to report that some methods have many dependencies. This way, without support, developers are likely to introduce similar problems to the ones we describe in this chapter. In addition, notice that dependencies regarding the #elif,

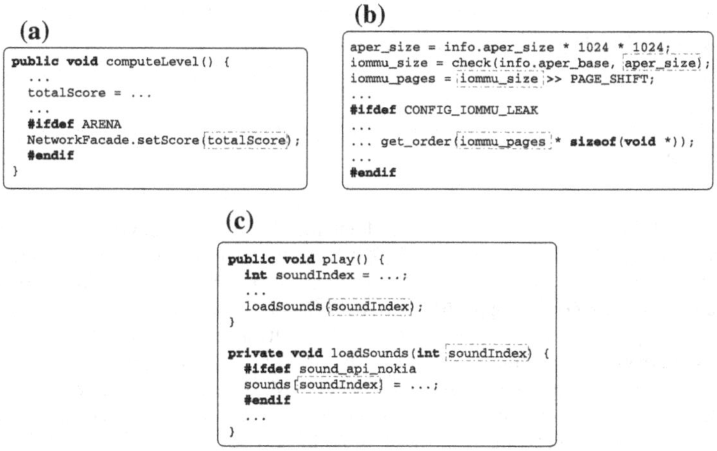

Fig. 3.6 Dependencies from *Best Lap*, *Kernel*, and *Juggling*, respectively. **a** Simple dependency. **b** Chain of assignments. **c** Interprocedural

Table 3.2 Some dependencies per method and per preprocessor directive of the *berkeley db* family

File.Method	#elif	#elifdef	#elifndef	#else	#if	#ifdef	#ifndef
select.sqlite3Select	0	0	0	0	28	0	25
sqlite3.ChooseLeaf	0	0	0	0	22	0	0
mutex_unix.pthreadMutexEnter	0	0	0	1	2	11	0
sqlite3.btreeCompare	0	0	0	0	0	0	9
expr.sqlite3ExprAlloc	0	0	0	0	1	0	0
lempar.yy_pop_parser_stack	0	0	0	0	0	0	2
b_del.b_del	0	0	0	3	3	0	0
expr.codeInteger	0	0	0	4	0	3	0
impexp.table_dump	0	0	0	5	5	0	0
os_unix.fillInUnixFile	0	0	0	0	42	0	0
sqlite3odbc.drvconnect	0	0	0	0	5	0	0
sqlite3.sqlite3_wal_autocheckpoint	0	0	0	0	0	0	4
sqlite3.yy_pop_parser_stack	0	0	0	0	0	0	2
blobtoxy.b2xy_filter	0	0	0	9	4	0	0
vtab.sqlite3VtabBeginParse	0	0	0	0	0	0	7
test1.test_rekey	0	0	0	0	0	3	0
shell.open_db	0	0	0	0	0	0	1
fts2.sqlite3Fts2Init	0	0	0	0	0	1	0
os_unix.unixCurrentTimeInt64	2	0	0	2	2	2	0
test6.Sqlitetest6_Init	0	0	0	0	0	0	5
sqlite3.sqlite3VdbeFreeCursor	0	0	0	0	0	0	5
sqlite3.resolveCompoundOrderBy	0	0	0	0	3	0	0
sqlite3.sqlite3VdbeMemTranslate	0	0	0	0	2	0	0
sqlite3.sqlite3Init	0	0	0	0	0	0	8

`#elifdef`, and `#elifndef` directives are not common. Although we do not show here, this holds for the other software families as well.

References

1. Figueiredo, E., Cacho, N., Sant'Anna, C., Monteiro, M., Kulesza, U., Garcia, A., Soares, S., Ferrari, F., Khan, S., Filho, F., Dantas, F.: Evolving software product lines with aspects: an empirical study on design stability. In: Proceedings of the 30th International Conference on Software Engineering (ICSE), pp. 261–270. ACM (2008)
2. Kästner, C., Apel, S., Kuhlemann, M.: Granularity in software product lines. In: Proceedings of the 30th International Conference on Software Engineering (ICSE), pp. 311–320. ACM (2008)
3. Liebig, J., Apel, S., Lengauer, C., Kästner, C., Schulze, M.: An analysis of the variability in forty preprocessor-based software product lines. In: Proceedings of the 32nd International Conference on Software Engineering (ICSE), pp. 105–114, ACM (2010)

4. Parnas, D.L.: On the criteria to be used in decomposing systems into modules. CACM **15**(12), 1053–1058 (1972)
5. Ribeiro, M., Queiroz, F., Borba, P., Tolêdo, T., Brabrand, C., Soares, S.: On the impact of feature dependencies when maintaining preprocessor-based software product lines. In: Proceedings of the 10th International Conference on Generative Programming and Component Engineering (GPCE), pp. 23–32, ACM (2011)
6. Wulf, W., Shaw, M.: Global variable considered harmful. SIGPLAN Not. **8**(2), 28–34 (1973)

Chapter 4
Emergent Feature Modularization

Abstract This chapter illustrates our proposal named Emergent Interfaces. To better illustrate how our interfaces work, we revisit the problematic scenarios of Chap. 3. Then, we show the general idea and how we compute dependencies. Afterwards, we explain our proposal to compute dependencies based on dataflow analyses, making such analyses feature sensitive. Then, we show how to use feature-sensitive analyses to compute Emergent Interfaces and the tool support named Emergo. Last but not least, we improve the expressiveness of Emergent Interfaces by using contracts and then illustrate how we can apply Emergent Interfaces in other mechanisms apart from preprocessors.

Keywords Emergent interfaces · Feature-sensitive dataflow analyses · Control-flow graph · Lattice · Transfer functions · Emergo · Contracts · Aspect-oriented programming

To solve the previously discussed problems, we propose an approach named Emergent Interfaces [14, 15]. The idea consists of establishing, on demand and according to a given maintenance task, interfaces for feature implementations. Such interfaces are neither predefined nor have a rigid structure. Developers do not need to write them. Instead, they *emerge* to give support for specific feature maintenance tasks, allowing us to change a feature abstracting details of the surrounding feature code. Emergent Interfaces alert the developer about potential features she might impact with the maintenance task. With this information, she is aware of feature dependencies and then can avoid introducing problems into other features. To do so, Emergent Interfaces basically capture dependencies between the feature we are maintaining and the others.

Emergent Interfaces might rely on feature models. This means we can take only valid feature combinations into account, preventing developers from reasoning about feature constraints and even from assuming invalid dependencies in case of mutually exclusive features (which may cause potential errors).

To better illustrate how Emergent Interfaces work, we revisit in Sect. 4.1 the three scenarios we show in Chap. 3. Then, we present a definition to Emergent Interfaces (Sect. 4.2) and discuss the general idea of our approach by using a conceptual model in Sect. 4.3. Because Emergent Interfaces must capture feature dependencies, dataflow analyses must take features into consideration. However, instead of generating all

© The Author(s) 2014
M. Ribeiro et al., *Emergent Interfaces for Feature Modularization*,
SpringerBriefs in Computer Science, DOI 10.1007/978-3-319-11493-4_4

possible products (of a product line, for example) and analyzing them individually, we make dataflow analysis feature sensitive [3, 4] (Sect. 4.4). We then show how we read the feature-sensitive analysis information to generate and show Emergent Interfaces for developers (Sect. 4.5) and present Emergo in Sect. 4.6, a tool for computing Emergent Interfaces. Finally, we improve the expressiveness of Emergent Interfaces by taking contracts into account (Sect. 4.7) and discuss in Sect. 4.8 how we can use Emergent Interfaces in other mechanisms apart from preprocessors.

4.1 Maintenance Features (Revisited)

Firstly, we show how Emergent Interfaces work in **Scenario 1** (Sect. 3.1.1), where a developer changed the value of the `totalScore` variable. The first step when using Emergent Interfaces consists of selecting the *maintenance points*, here only the `totalScore` assignment (see the dashed rectangle in Fig. 4.1). Then, we execute a dataflow analysis to capture the dependencies between the feature we are maintaining and the other ones. Finally, the interface emerges. Notice that the interfaces are able to show the sets of features (configurations) that our maintenance may impact.

The interface states in Fig. 4.1 that the maintenance may impact products that contain the *arena* feature. In other words, we *provide* the actual `totalScore` value to the *arena* feature. Now, the developer is aware of the dependency. Reading the interface is important for **Scenario 1**, since the emerged information alerts the developer that she should also analyze the *arena* feature. Probably, when analyzing it, she would discover she must also change *arena*, avoiding **Error introduction**.

Besides *arena*, notice that the code might have many other features with their own dependencies, making code navigation difficult. Emergent Interfaces help to reduce **Effort**, since they indicate precisely the configurations we should analyze. To achieve this, Emergent Interfaces rely on feature-sensitive dataflow analysis [15], detailed in Sect. 4.4. This means that our analyses take feature combinations into consideration. We also consider feature constraints information. For example, if we are maintaining feature *A*, there is no need to consider feature *B* in the interface when they are mutually exclusive. In other words, the maintenance in feature *A* does not impact feature *B* at all.

This way, our interfaces focus on the configurations that we indeed might impact, freeing developers from the task of analyzing unnecessary features, minimizing **Effort**. For instance, consider **Scenario 2** (Sect. 3.1.2) in which we use the

Fig. 4.1 Emergent interface
for Scenario 1

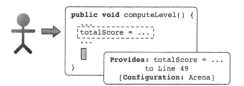

Fig. 4.2 Emergent interface
for Scenario 2

status variable in two optional features. In this context, our interface—illustrated
in Fig. 4.2—ignores the *black* feature, since it does not use the status variable.
Now, the navigation throughout the code is easier. Besides, we are now aware of
two features that use the status variable, so we probably would encompass the
variable declaration with the two colors that correspond to such features. Therefore,
we can again minimize **Error introduction**.

Analogously, Emergent Interfaces help us in **Scenario 3** (Sect. 3.1.3) since they
would make developers aware of the use of the error variable in the optional *PDF*
feature.

4.2 Definition

We now give a definition for Emergent Interfaces. An Emergent Interface is an abstraction of the data dependencies of a particular feature [13]. The interface contains
a set of provides and requires clauses that describe such dependencies. These clauses
express dependencies according to def-use chains. In this case, features might introduce definitions used by other features (and vice-versa). In other words, Emergent
Interfaces make explicit that a particular feature requires data from others and, at the
same time, provides data to others.

4.3 General Idea

After revisiting each scenario and discussing how Emergent Interfaces help on avoiding feature maintenance problems, we now show the general idea of our approach.

As discussed, we generate Emergent Interfaces according to the feature code we
are supposed to maintain (the maintenance points). Developers select these points
and then, after some computation, the interface emerges. We denote the feature code
to maintain by component, named *Selection*. The backward/forward paths of the
code surrounding it are components as well. Paths consider the different feature
combinations according to the feature constraints. We name these paths *Dataflows*,
since features exchange data among them. Emergent Interfaces basically capture data

Fig. 4.3 Components and
their respective interfaces

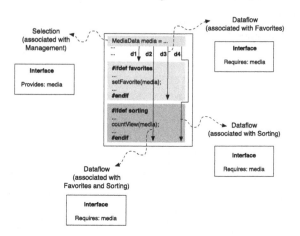

dependencies between these components, and give support for maintaining *Selection* without having to understand the details of code associated to the *Dataflows*.

To illustrate these components, consider the following example from *MobileMedia* [6], which is a product line with about 3KLOC that manipulates photos, musics, and videos on mobile devices. The example contains two optional features, *Sorting* and *Favorites*, and a mandatory one, *Management*. We should maintain the `media` variable declared in the *Management* feature. So, in this particular case, our *Selection* component consists of the `media` declaration. Figure 4.3 illustrates forward *Dataflows* with arrows. Since *Sorting* and *Favorites* are optional features, there are four sets of features, each one associated with a *Dataflow* component:

- **d1**: {*Management*};
- **d2**: {*Management, Favorites, Sorting*};
- **d3**: {*Management, Favorites*}; and
- **d4**: {*Management, Sorting*}.

Notice that we use sets of features instead of feature expressions. Although the latter is more general, we use the former to more easily explain our ideas and keep consistency throughout the work. Back to the example, for each component (*Selection* and *Dataflow*), we compute associated interfaces expressing dependencies between them. For example, Fig. 4.3 shows that the *Dataflow d3* (associated with *Favorites*) requires the `media` variable provided by the *Selection* component. Notice that these interfaces allow us to change *Selection* abstracting details of the surrounding feature code. At the same time, they provide information to the developer, so she might avoid changes that cause problems to other features, like removing `media`, for example.

An advantage of using feature constraints is that we can remove invalid dataflows. For instance, suppose we associate the *Selection* component with feature *A*, that cannot be present in the same product with feature *B*. This might be due to a constraint in the feature model or by them being alternative features. Therefore, we can safely discard dataflows containing both features.

Fig. 4.4 Conceptual model
of our approach

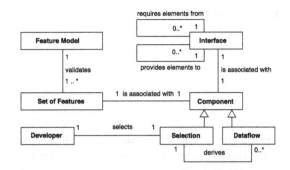

To summarize these ideas, we depict the conceptual model of our approach in Fig. 4.4. As explained, there are two kinds of components: *Selection*, which corresponds to the feature code to maintain (selected by the developer); and *Dataflow*, representing dataflows derived from the *Selection* component. The *Dataflows* are useful to navigate through the code, being important to retrieve data dependencies among features with respect to the *Selection*. For example, through *Dataflow d4*, we learn that the *Sorting* feature uses `media`, which is a variable declared in the *Selection*. We discard the *Dataflow* in which all code is only associated with the *Selection* set of features. This way, *d1* (Fig. 4.3) is not taken into consideration. So, as mentioned, we associate each component with a set of features and an interface, which states that components may provide/require elements such as variables to/from other components. These interfaces emerge from the components, establishing contracts between the feature implementations.

In this work we use the following notion of interface: "an interface is a way to resolve potential conflicts between interacting parts of a design" [2]. Here, we need to resolve conflicts between features caused by feature dependencies. So, we have a treaty between two or more features. To minimize the conflicts, we emerge interfaces and make the affected parties aware of dependencies. To do so and then provide better support during feature maintenance, our interfaces contain *provide/require* information with respect to the feature we are maintaining and the others. This way, as long as developers respect the interface (which should be the less likely artifact to change, otherwise communication between the developers would be necessary), they can avoid conflicts and then evolve the system in parallel [2].

4.4 Feature-Sensitive Analysis

In this chapter, we discuss that Emergent Interfaces provide information taking feature combinations into consideration. This is important because we can generate interfaces that provide precise information about the configurations we might indeed impact due to our maintenance task. To recover the interface information, we can actually use conventional dataflow analysis. In this way, we generate all possible

Fig. 4.5 Increase and decrease toy SPL

```
void m() {
  int x = 0;
  #ifdef A
  x++;
  #endif
  #ifdef B
  x--;
  #endif
}
```

configurations within a method—all method variants—and analyze them individually. However, the costs to generate the interfaces by using this feature-oblivious analysis is high, specially in case of many features within a method.

To minimize the costs, we propose two approaches to avoid the generation of all possible method variants [3, 4]. So, instead of using the feature-oblivious approach, we make *intraprocedural* dataflow analysis feature sensitive. In fact, we propose two ways in which this can be done; *consecutive* and *simultaneous* feature-sensitive analysis. Both achieve cost gains, as we shall see in Sect. 5.3. When using the former, there is no need to generate and compile all possible method variants. Besides these gains, the latter needs only one fixed-point computation (instead of multiple computations, one for each method variant).

We illustrate each approach using the sign analysis presented in Sect. 2.2. By using the toy SPL depicted in Fig. 4.5 as our running example, we show the feature-oblivious approach (Sect. 4.4.1) and then we move towards the feature-sensitive approach (Sects. 4.4.2 and 4.4.3).

The SPL uses features $\mathbb{F} = \{A, B\}$ and we assume it has a feature model $\psi_{\text{FM}} = A \vee B$. By using this feature model, we have the following set of valid configurations: $[\![\psi_{\text{FM}}]\!] = \{\{A\}, \{B\}, \{A, B\}\}$.

4.4.1 Feature-Oblivious Analysis—Brute Force ($\mathscr{A}$1)

We may analyze software families and product lines *intraprocedurally* by building *all* possible methods. Then, we analyze them one by one using a conventional dataflow analysis as described in the previous section. In this context, a method with c number of features yields 2^c number of possible method variants (minus the ones invalidated by feature constraints). Figure 4.6 illustrates that, for our tiny method that has features A and B, we have to build and analyze three distinct methods.

```
c = {A}
void m() {
  int x = 0;
  x++;
}
```

```
c = {B}
void m() {
  int x = 0;
  x--;
}
```

```
c = {A,B}
void m() {
  int x = 0;
  x++;
  x--;
}
```

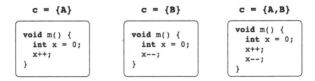

Fig. 4.6 Each possible product of our toy SPL

Depending on the number of features, this process can be costly. We now show two approaches ($\mathscr{A}2$ and $\mathscr{A}3$) to analyze software families and product lines in a better way while staying within the framework of dataflow analysis.

4.4.2 Consecutive Feature-Sensitive Analysis ($\mathscr{A}2$)

By making a dataflow analysis feature sensitive, we avoid explicitly building all methods individually. Now, considering only disciplined annotations, we show how to take any single-program dataflow analysis and automatically turn it into a feature-sensitive analysis, capable of analyzing all possible method variants. In fact, we propose two ways in which this can be done; *consecutive* or *simultaneous* feature-sensitive analysis of method variants. We now present the former; the latter is presented in the next section. One way of making the analysis feature sensitive is to instrument the CFG with sufficient information for the transfer functions to know whether a given statement is to be executed or not in each configuration.

4.4.2.1 Control-Flow Graph (CFG)

For each node in the CFG, we associate the *set of features*, $\{\phi\}$, for which its corresponding statement is executed. We refer to this process as *CFG instrumentation*. Figure 4.7 illustrates the CFG for the toy increase-decrease SPL.

We label the nodes with "$\{\phi\}$: S" where S is the statement and $\{\phi\}$ is the feature set associated with S. Unconditionally executed statements (mandatory statements, e.g., int x = 0;) have the empty set, $\{\}$, associated. Nested statements like S in "ifdef (ϕ_1) ifdef (ϕ_2) S" will have the set of features $\{\phi_1, \phi_2\}$ associated.

Fig. 4.7 Instrumented CFG

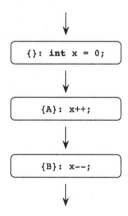

4.4.2.2 Lattice

When analyzing the configurations consecutively, we do not need to change the lattice. This way, the lattice of this feature-sensitive analysis is the same as that of the feature-oblivious analysis.

4.4.2.3 Transfer Functions

Now, all we need to do in the feature-sensitive transfer function is use the associated feature set, $\{\phi\}$, to figure out whether or not to execute the feature-oblivious transfer function, f_S, in a given configuration, c. In other words, we need to decide $\{\phi\} \subseteq c$.

4.4.2.4 Analysis

To analyze an SPL using $\mathscr{A}2$, all we have to do is to combine the CFG, lattice, and transfer functions. Figure 4.8 depicts the result of analyzing the increase-decrease SPL using this consecutive feature-sensitive analysis. As can be seen, the consecutive feature-sensitive analysis needs one fixed-point computation for each configuration. Differently from $\mathscr{A}1$, we do not need to compile every different configuration.

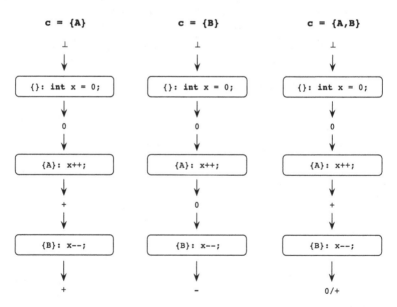

Fig. 4.8 Results of the consecutive analysis (on the increase-decrease SPL)

4.4.3 Simultaneous Feature-Sensitive Analysis ($\mathscr{A}3$)

Another approach consists of analyzing all configurations *simultaneously* by using a lifted lattice that maintains one lattice element per valid configuration. In contrast to the consecutive analysis, the simultaneous analysis needs only one fixed point computation. This simultaneous idea will be feature sensitive and it can also be automatically derived from the feature-oblivious analysis.

4.4.3.1 Control-Flow Graph

The CFG of $\mathscr{A}3$ is the same as that of $\mathscr{A}2$, which includes the necessary information for deciding whether or not to simulate execution of a conditional statement.

4.4.3.2 Lattice

As explained above, we lift the feature-oblivious lattice, $\mathscr{L}$. This way, it will have one element per valid configuration:

$$[\![\psi_{\mathrm{FM}}]\!] \to \mathscr{L}$$

In what follows, we present an example element of this lattice:

$$\{\{A\} \mapsto +, \{B\} \mapsto -, \{A, B\} \mapsto 0/-\} \quad \in \quad [\![\psi_{\mathrm{FM}}]\!] \to \mathscr{L}$$

corresponding to the following information: for configuration $\{A\}$, we know that the value of x is positive "+"; for $\{B\}$, we know x is negative "$-$"; and for $\{A, B\}$, we know it is zero-or-negative "$0/-$". Using the lifted lattice of the simultaneous analysis, it is possible to lazily share lattice values corresponding to configurations that are indistinguishable in the program being analyzed [3].

4.4.3.3 Transfer Functions

We lift the transfer functions so they work on elements of the lifted lattice in a pointwise manner. We apply the transfer functions only on the configurations for which the statement is executed. For instance, consider the statement "`#ifdef (A) x++;`". The effect of the lifted transfer function on the lattice element $\{\{A\} \mapsto 0, \{B\} \mapsto 0, \{A, B\} \mapsto 0\}$ is depicted in Fig. 4.9.

We apply the transfer function to each of the configurations for which the `#ifdef` formula A is satisfied. Since $\{A\} \subseteq \{A\}$ and $\{A\} \subseteq \{A, B\}$, the function is applied to the lattice values of the configurations $\{A\}$ and $\{A, B\}$ with resulting value:

Fig. 4.9 Effect of the lifted transfer function due the `#ifdef (A) x++;` statement

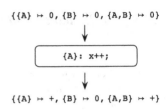

$f_{x++}(0) = +$. The same does not happen for configuration $\{B\}$, since it does not satisfy the formula $\{A\} \nsubseteq \{B\}$, so its value is left unchanged with value 0.

4.4.3.4 Analysis

Again, we combine the lifted CFG, lifted lattice, and lifted transfer functions to achieve our feature-sensitive simultaneous analysis. Figure 4.10 illustrates the result of analyzing the toy SPL using $\mathscr{A}3$.

When analyzing Fig. 4.10, we know the sign of the variable x at different program points, for each of the valid configurations. For example, at the end of the program in configuration $\{B\}$, we can see that x is always negative and, analogously, in configuration $\{A\}$, x is always positive.

When compared to $\mathscr{A}2$, this analysis only has one fixed-point iteration and thus potentially saves the overhead involved during the analysis execution. Nevertheless, it requires the maximum number of fixed-point iterations that are performed in any configuration of $\mathscr{A}2$ to reach its fixed-point because of the pointwise lifted lattice.

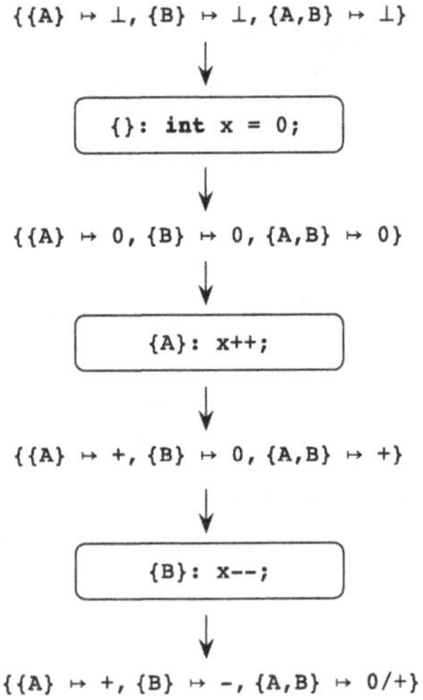

Fig. 4.10 Results of the simultaneous analysis (on the increase-decrease SPL)

```
{{A} ↦ ⊥, {B} ↦ ⊥, {A,B} ↦ ⊥}
                 ↓
        {}: int x = 0;
                 ↓
{{A} ↦ 0, {B} ↦ 0, {A,B} ↦ 0}
                 ↓
           {A}: x++;
                 ↓
{{A} ↦ +, {B} ↦ 0, {A,B} ↦ +}
                 ↓
           {B}: x--;
                 ↓
{{A} ↦ +, {B} ↦ -, {A,B} ↦ 0/+}
```

To perform *interprocedural* analyses, our lifted lattice should contain one element per valid configuration of the entire SPL. When reaching a method call, we bind the real parameters with the callee formal ones. Then we perform the *intraprocedural* analysis recursively within the callee method, exactly as we do within the caller method.

4.5 From Feature-Sensitive Dataflow Analyses to Emergent Interfaces

In this section we put all the discussed ideas together. We show how we generate Emergent Interfaces based on the feature-sensitive dataflow analysis.

To better explain this, we consider the example from the *Best Lap* product line illustrated in Sect. 3.1.1. Now, we extend the example and consider a new feature, *turbo*, responsible for increasing the car speed. The computation of the totalScore of this new feature is completely different from the normal one. It depends on the turbo usage during the race. In this way, as depicted in Fig. 4.11, we now have two mutually exclusive computations for totalScore; one with the normal configuration (i.e., {*Normal*}); and one with turbo (i.e., {*Turbo*}).

Now, suppose the developer needs to change the way of computing totalScore in {*Normal*}. Because we use totalScore in both *turbo* and *arena* features, our interface could inform she might impact the following configurations: (i) *turbo*; (ii) *arena*; and (iii) *turbo and arena*. However, as we shall see throughout this section, we discard two configurations (i and iii). Firstly, according to the standard reaching definitions [11] dataflow analysis, the assignment we are changing does not reach the use of totalScore in *turbo* (see the nextLevelAvailTurbos assignment), since it is killed within the if and else statements. Secondly, if we consider feature-sensitive dataflow analysis, again the assignment does not reach the use in *turbo* since, according to the feature constraint in Fig. 4.11, the feature we are changing (*normal*) and *turbo* are mutually exclusive.

Now that we introduced the example, we execute the feature-sensitive dataflow analysis (Sect. 4.5.1) and then we use the results to generate the Emergent Interfaces (Sect. 4.5.2). Although we focus on techniques we use in this book, this separation is

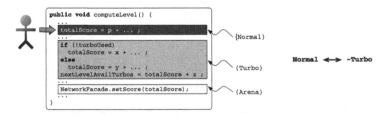

Fig. 4.11 Two mutually exclusive computations for totalScore

important to make clear that there are other ways to perform each part. For example, instead of dataflow analyses, we might navigate throughout the AST to capture dependencies. Then, we can use the impacted AST nodes as elements of our Emergent Interface.

4.5.1 Executing Feature-Sensitive Dataflow Analyses

To generate Emergent Interfaces, the first step consists of executing feature-sensitive dataflow analyses within the target method. For this particular example, we consider the feature-sensitive reaching definitions analysis, so our lattices contain assignments. Figure 4.12 illustrates the results of this analysis for each valid configuration. Also, notice that we shrink the original variable names to better illustrate and explain the results.

According to the general emergent approach presented in Sect. 4.3, we represent each valid configuration as a *Dataflow* component (see the legend part of Fig. 4.12). This is consistent with the ideas explained in Sect. 4.4, where we have one lattice per valid configuration. In its turn, the lifted lattice groups all lattices. As can be seen, we illustrate one lifted lattice for each statement of our example. Notice that here the *Selection* component has not been defined yet.

As mentioned, we execute the feature-sensitive reaching definitions analysis, so the analysis already assigns values to the lifted lattices. For example, due to the execution of $tS = p$, since such a statement is instrumented as {*Normal*}, we applied the transfer functions only to lattices of the configurations {*Normal, Arena*} and {*Normal*}, as detailed in what follows:

- **(d1)** {*Normal, Arena*}: applied, because {*Normal*} $\subseteq$ {*Normal, Arena*};
- **(d2)** {*Turbo, Arena*}: not applied, because {*Normal*} $\not\subseteq$ {*Turbo, Arena*};
- **(d3)** {*Normal*}: applied, because {*Normal*} $\subseteq$ {*Normal*};
- **(d4)** {*Turbo*}: not applied, because {*Normal*} $\not\subseteq$ {*Turbo*}.

Method code	Lifted Lattice
{N}: tS = p;	{{N,A} ↦ {tS = p}, {T,A} ↦ {}, {N} ↦ {tS = p}, {T} ↦ {}}
...	{{N,A} ↦ {tS = p}, {T,A} ↦ {}, {N} ↦ {tS = p}, {T} ↦ {}}
{T}: if (!turbo)	{{N,A} ↦ {tS = p}, {T,A} ↦ {}, {N} ↦ {tS = p}, {T} ↦ {}}
{T}: tS = x;	{{N,A} ↦ {tS = p}, {T,A} ↦ {tS = x}, {N} ↦ {tS = p}, {T} ↦ {tS = x}}
{T}: else	
{T}: tS = y;	{{N,A} ↦ {tS = p}, {T,A} ↦ {tS = x/y}, {N} ↦ {tS = p}, {T} ↦ {tS = x/y}}
{T}: n = tS+z;	{{N,A} ↦ {tS = p}, {T,A} ↦ {tS = x/y, n = tS+z}, {N} ↦ {tS = p}, {T} ↦ {tS = x/y, n = tS+z}}
...	{{N,A} ↦ {tS = p}, {T,A} ↦ {tS = x/y, n = tS+z}, {N} ↦ {tS = p}, {T} ↦ {tS = x/y, n = tS+z}}
{A}: setScore(tS);	{{N,A} ↦ {tS = p}, {T,A} ↦ {tS = x/y, n = tS+z}, {N} ↦ {tS = p}, {T} ↦ {tS = x/y, n = tS+z}}

Valid Configurations:
d1 = {N,A} = {Normal, Arena}
d2 = {T,A} = {Turbo, Arena}
d3 = {N}:   = {Normal}
d4 = {T}:   = {Turbo}

Fig. 4.12 Results of the feature-sensitive reaching definitions analysis. Typically we associate lattice information with edges, not nodes. So, the lattice information here corresponds to the edge right after the statement node

In the reaching definitions analysis, applying the transfer function means executing the *gen* and *kill* functions, discussed in Sect. 2.2.2. So, our lattices have assignments. For our particular example, this explains why we include `tS = p` in the lattices.

Notice that when features are not taken into account by the reaching definitions analysis, `tS = p` does not reach the `setScore(tS)` statement at all. This happens because `tS = x` and `tS = y` kill `tS = p`. On the other hand, when using our feature-sensitive approach, `tS = p` reaches the `setScore(tS)` statement for the configuration {*Normal, Arena*}.

4.5.2 Generating Emergent Interfaces

After executing the analysis, we need to cross the results with the *Selection* component. In our particular example, such a component consists of the `tS = p` assignment in the *Normal* feature. So, we need to investigate, for each configuration, if the assignment `tS = p` reaches a point in the code that uses the `tS` variable. In other words—as explained in Sect. 4.3—since we denote each valid configuration as a *Dataflow* component, we verify which ones require the `tS` value that the *Selection* component provides. If these components match, we consider them in the interface. However, this is not enough since the *Selection* feature must make sense—according to the feature model—together with the *Dataflow* component.

Our algorithm to generate Emergent Interfaces begins taking all assignments of the *Selection* component; all configurations of the lifted lattice; and all statements of the target method. To easily explain the algorithm, we consider only two configurations of our example: {*Normal, Arena*} and {*Normal*}. Our target method is `computeLevel` and the *Selection* component consists of the `tS = p` assignment. Therefore, we have three nested loops: (i) for the *Selection* assignments; (ii) for the configurations; and (iii) for the method statements. Inside the innermost loop, we verify three conditions. To explain them, we use concrete values for assignments, configurations, and statements. In particular, we consider four cases:

- **Case 1**:

  - Assignment = `tS = p`;
  - Configuration = {*Normal, Arena*};
  - Statement = `n = tS + z`.

- **Case 2**:

  - Assignment = `tS = p`;
  - Configuration = {*Turbo, Arena*};
  - Statement = `n = tS + z`.

Method code	Lifted Lattice
{N}: tS = p; ...	{{N,A} ↦ {tS = p}, {T,A} ↦ {}, {N} ↦ {tS = p}, {T} ↦ {}} {{N,A} ↦ {tS = p}, {T,A} ↦ {}, {N} ↦ {tS = p}, {T} ↦ {}}
{T}: if (!turbo) {T}: tS = x; {T}: else	{{N,A} ↦ {tS = p}, {T,A} ↦ {}, {N} ↦ {tS = p}, {T} ↦ {}} {{N,A} ↦ {tS = p}, {T,A} ↦ {tS = x}, {N} ↦ {tS = p}, {T} ↦ {tS = x}}
{T}: tS = y; {T}: n = tS+z; ...	{{N,A} ↦ {tS = p}, {T,A} ↦ {tS = x/y}, {N} ↦ {tS = p}, {T} ↦ {tS = x/y}} {{N,A} ↦ {tS = p}, {T,A} ↦ {tS = x/y, n = tS+z}, {N} ↦ {tS = p}, {T} ↦ {tS = x/y, n = tS+z}} {{N,A} ↦ {tS = p}, {T,A} ↦ {tS = x/y, n = tS+z}, {N} ↦ {tS = p}, {T} ↦ {tS = x/y, n = tS+z}}
{A}: setScore(tS);	{{N,A} ↦ {tS = p}, {T,A} ↦ {tS = x/y, n = tS+z}, {N} ↦ {tS = p}, {T} ↦ {tS = x/y, n = tS+z}}

Fig. 4.13 Focusing on some statements and configurations to better explain our algorithm

- **Case 3**:

  - Assignment = tS = p;
  - Configuration = {*Normal, Arena*};
  - Statement = setScore(tS).

- **Case 4**:

  - Assignment = tS = p;
  - Configuration = {*Normal*};
  - Statement = setScore(tS).

We detach each case in Fig. 4.13.

As mentioned, we verify three conditions. First, we verify whether the set of features $\{\phi\}$ of the selected statements is a subset of the configuration being analyzed. This condition is important because if it is not a subset, we can discard the statement and move towards the next one. For example, in **Case 1**, since the statement n = tS + z is instrumented as {*Turbo*}, we verify if {*Turbo*} ⊆ {*Normal, Arena*}. Because it is not a subset, this statement makes no sense for the current configuration. The same happens for **Case 4**, since {*Arena*} ⊄ {*Normal*}.

The second condition verifies if $\{\phi\} \cup \{\alpha\} \in [\![\psi_{FM}]\!]$, where $\{\phi\}$ is the set of features of the statement being analyzed and $\{\alpha\}$ is the set of features of the assignment. The first condition is true for **Case 2**, since {*Turbo*} ⊆ {*Turbo, Arena*}. However, the second condition is false, because {*Turbo*} ∪ {*Normal*} ∉ $[\![\psi_{FM}]\!]$. We need this condition to avoid interfaces that indicate we might impact a feature that is alternative to the one we are maintaining. As discussed, both features will never be together in the same product.

The third condition verifies if the assignment reaches the statement for the current configuration. If all conditions are true, we generate the Emergent Interface. This happens for **Case 3**. The third condition is true since the assignment tS = p reaches the statement setScore(tS) when considering the configuration {*Normal, Arena*}. We can see this information in the lattice of the statement setScore(tS) for this configuration: {*Normal, Arena*} ↦ $\{tS = p\}$. We summarize all these ideas in Algorithm 1.

Therefore, according to the algorithm, the only configuration we might impact when maintaining the tS = p assignment is {*Normal, Arena*}. Since we already

Algorithm 1 General algorithm for generating Emergent Interfaces from feature-sensitive reaching definitions analysis.

ASSIGNMENTS ← set of assignments within the *Selection* component
STATEMENTS ← set of all statements within the method where the selection occurred
CONFIGURATIONS ← set of all possible configurations
FEATURES(s) ← function that returns the set of features associated with statement s
REACHES(a, s, c) ← function that returns true, if the assignment a reaches the statement s in configuration c; and false, otherwise
FEATURE MODEL ← set with sets of valid features
INTERFACE DATA ← set of entries for the Emergent Interface
STORE(a, s, c) ← function that stores the results in INTERFACE DATA

for each assignment in ASSIGNMENTS **do**
  for each configuration in CONFIGURATIONS **do**
    for each statement in STATEMENTS **do**
      if FEATURES(statement) ⊆ configuration **then**
        if (FEATURES(statement) ∪ FEATURES(assignment)) ∈ FEATURE MODEL
        then
          if REACHES(assignment, statement, configuration) **then**
            STORE(configuration,assignment,statement) in INTERFACE DATA
          end if
        end if
      end if
    end for
  end for
end for

Fig. 4.14 Emergent interface generated after selecting the tS = p assignment

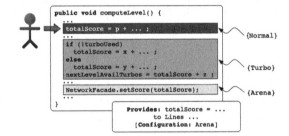

know we are maintaining {*Normal*}, we might remove this feature (the feature from the *Selection* component) before showing the interface (see Fig. 4.14).

We now briefly analyze the complexity of our algorithm. Let a and s be the set of selected assignments and statements within a method m, respectively. If the developer selects everything, we have $s = a$, but usually we have $s > a$. Let c be the number of configurations within m. Assuming that the three nested if statements execute in constant time O(1) (we can precompute the feature model and use bitwise operations and hash tables to apply ⊆, ∪, and ∈), our algorithm is O(c.n^2). This is the worst case, where we execute the three nested for statements n, c, and n

times, respectively. The best case happens when the set a has only one element (the developer selected only one assignment). In this case, we have $O(c.n.1)$, which boils down to $O(c.n)$.

4.6 Supporting Developers with Emergo

To support developers with Emergent Interfaces, we implemented a prototype tool [16, 17] based on Eclipse plug-ins [5]. We call this tool "Emergo", that means "emerge" in Latin. Emergo can compute Emergent Interfaces based on feature dependencies between methods or within a single method, by using *interprocedural* or *intraprocedural* dataflow analysis, respectively. In summary, Emergo takes the following feature dependencies into consideration:

- Simple (see Fig. 3.6a);
- Chain of Assignments (see Fig. 3.6b);
- Interprocedural (see Fig. 3.6c).

To generate Emergent Interfaces, the developer firstly selects the maintenance points and then invokes the tool for the interfaces. Figure 4.15 presents a screenshot of Emergo. The developer is maintaining the base code. She selects `int totalScore = perfectCurvesCounter * ..` as the maintenance point. The *Emergo Table View* presents the Emergent Interface as a table (see the bottom of Fig. 4.15) and the *Emergo Graph View* presents the interface as a graph (see the right-hand side of Fig. 4.15).

Fig. 4.15 Emergo

Fig. 4.16 Emergo properties screen

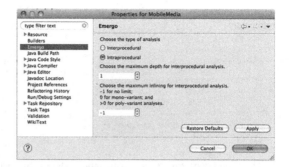

Both views (table and graph) present all configurations we might impact if we change the maintenance points. In this way, developers can analyze the interface and then proceed with the maintenance task, but now aware of the dependencies. In addition, developers can navigate throughout the code using both views by clicking on any interface element. After the click, the editor moves the cursor to the class and source line that represents such an element.

In our particular example, changing the `totalScore` value can potentially impact products containing the `ARENA` feature. This happens because `ARENA` uses `totalScore`.

Emergo also provides a properties screen where developers can choose between *intraprocedural* and *interprocedural* analyses (see Fig. 4.16). Moreover, developers can set the method call depth used during the interface computation. When decreasing this value, developers exchange precision for performance, leading Emergo to generate interfaces faster. However, since we define the maximum depth, the interface generated might miss important feature dependencies.

4.6.1 Feature Model

Emergo uses feature model information to compute Emergent Interfaces. By using the feature model, Emergo does not compute dependencies based on invalid config-urations. Therefore, we avoid false positives, which means that we might invalidate some feature dependencies based on the feature model information. To set the feature model of an Eclipse project, developers must create an `ifdef.txt`. In this file, we write the available features as well as the feature constraints. For example, to define that features *A* and *B* are alternative, we may write A $<=>$!B.

4.6.2 Architecture

Figure 4.17 depicts the architecture of our tool. In this section, we detail each element of the architecture.

Fig. 4.17 Emergo
architecture

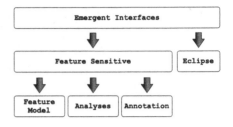

The *Emergent Interfaces* component depends on the *Feature Sensitive* component to execute dataflow analyses in a feature-sensitive way. The *Feature Sensitive*
component then executes feature-sensitive *Analyses* based on the Experimental Java
Compiler [18]. However, such a component needs to identify which code elements
are encompassed by which features. We extract this information by using the *Annotation* component. Internally, the *Annotation* component instruments the AST nodes
with feature information. We then retrieve this information from the instrumented
AST to feed the *Feature Sensitive* component to proceed with the analyses [3, 18].
The *Feature Sensitive* component also uses *Feature Model* information during the
feature-sensitive analyses to avoid analyzing invalid configurations.

After computing dataflow analysis for each configuration, we generate the Emergent Interfaces. The *Emergent Interfaces* component is responsible for this task. The
first step consists of reading the information computed by the *Feature Sensitive* component to obtain dataflow information for each possible configuration. Then, Emergo
computes the interface by crossing the obtained information with the maintenance
points. The result consists of a graph of dependencies that associates the maintenance points with points we might impact by changing the formers. Finally, Emergo
displays the interface to the developer in both Eclipse views.

4.7 Improving Expressiveness

Emergent Interfaces might reduce effort because they precisely point to the features (and configurations) the developer should check during a maintenance task.
Back to the *arena* example, notice however that the interface "Feature Arena
requires totalScore" does not provide any additional information regarding totalScore (such as the range of valid values for this variable), leading the
developer to still open and analyze the features pointed by the interface. This task
of analyzing features that are potentially not under the developer's responsibility
hinders modularity, which aims at achieving independent changeability and comprehensibility [12].

To minimize this problem, we improve the expressiveness of Emergent Interfaces. To do so, we might capture semantic information from the features by using contracts previously written in languages such as Java Modelling Language

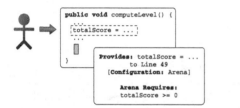

Fig. 4.18 Improving the expressiveness of emergent interfaces by using contracts

(JML) [10]. Figure 4.18 illustrates how this works. In this particular case, we are using the `requires` JML clause, that specifies the precondition of the `setScore` method (called by the `computeLevel` method). This way, we use this precondition to enhance the Emergent Interface, in the sense we now have semantic information regarding the `totalScore` variable. Now, the developer is aware not only that the *arena* feature requires `totalScore`, but that such a feature also requires `totalScore` to be positive.

Notice that this semantic information helps on achieving independent changeability. Now, when changing the `totalScore` assignment, she is aware of the `totalScore` valid range (`totalScore` $\geq$ 0). In case she desires to keep this contract, she do not need to open and analyze the *arena* feature, which is potentially not under her responsibility. Otherwise, she must change the contract. Consequently, checking and changing the *arena* feature is unavoidable.[1]

Formalizing the computation of Emergent Interfaces by considering contracts is out of the scope of this book. We intend to do so as future work.

4.8 Emergent Interfaces in Other Mechanisms

Emergent Interfaces help developers to avoid problems related to feature dependencies. Although we focus on preprocessors, the technique of emerging interfaces is general, which means we can apply it in other contexts, like product lines based on aspect-oriented programming, configuration files, components, and so forth. In what follows, we illustrate how we can use Emergent Interfaces in other mechanisms. We first focus on aspects and then on configuration files.

Aspect-oriented programming is a well-known mechanism that allows the separation of crosscutting concerns [9]. These concerns usually do not fit into one specific module, leading to scattering and tangling. When considering software families and product lines, features are commonly scattered and tangled with each other, so that aspects become useful to implement and separate them from the base code. Figure 4.19 illustrates a scenario where two aspects implement features *A* and *B* and

---

[1] Notice that this idea fits into ordinary interfaces as well. Changing the interfaces imply changing their clients.

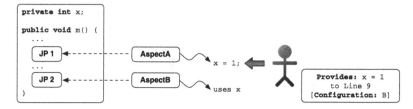

Fig. 4.19 Using emergent interface for aspects

Fig. 4.20 Using emergent interfaces for configuration files

intercept two different joinpoints. We have a developer that is supposed to change the value of x in A. Notice that there is a dataflow regarding x from feature A to feature B. This way, an Emergent Interface might warn the developer she might break feature B, since this feature uses the x global variable.

Another mechanism useful to implement software families and product lines is configuration files. Configuration Files are useful to separate the source code from values that may change the behavior from one version of the application to another [1]. Each value of the configuration file is mapped to a parameter. When executing, the application loads the configuration files and searches for the respective values of the source code parameters.

Figure 4.20 depicts a mapping between parameters and values and two configuration files (one for each alternative feature, i.e., *opera browser* and *motorola browser*), extracted from the Test Automation Framework (TAF), an object-oriented framework developed by Motorola Industrial that supports the creation of automated test cases for mobile phone software [7, 8].

The alternative features expect that the methods loadWebSession, access-URL, and saveInCache can deal with their configuration values. In this case, a maintenance may introduce problems when testing the features. For example, a given maintenance can let one of these three methods not prepared for a specific parameter value. In this situation, an Emergent Interface might be helpful to warn the developer about the configuration files that define such a parameter.

References

1. Alves, V.: Implementing software product line adoption strategies. Ph.D. thesis, Federal University of Pernambuco (2007)
2. Baldwin, C.Y., Clark, K.B.: Design Rules, Volume 1: The Power of Modularity. The MIT Press, Cambridge (2000)
3. Brabrand, C., Ribeiro, M., Tolêdo, T., Borba, P.: Intraprocedural dataflow analysis for software product lines. In: Proceedings of the 11th International Conference on Aspect-Oriented Software Development (AOSD), pp. 13–24. ACM (2012)
4. Brabrand, C., Ribeiro, M., Tolêdo, T., Winther, J., Borba, P.: Intraprocedural dataflow analysis for software product lines. In: Lecture Notes in Computer Science: Transactions on Aspect-Oriented Software Development I, pp. 73–108. Springer (2012)
5. Clayberg, E., Rubel, D.: Eclipse: Building Commercial-Quality Plug-ins. Addison-Wesley Professional, Reading (2006)
6. Figueiredo, E., Cacho, N., Sant'Anna, C., Monteiro, M., Kulesza, U., Garcia, A., Soares, S., Ferrari, F., Khan, S., Filho, F., Dantas, F.: Evolving software product lines with aspects: an empirical study on design stability. In: Proceedings of the 30th International Conference on Software Engineering (ICSE), pp. 261–270. ACM (2008)
7. Kawakami, L., Knabben, A., Rechia, D., Bastos, D., Pereira, O., Silva, R., Santos, L.: An object-oriented framework for improving software reuse on automated testing of mobile phones. In: Proceedings of Testing of Software and Communicating Systems—19th IFIP TC6/WG6.1 International Conference (TestCom), 7th International Workshop (FATES), pp. 199–211. Springer (2007)
8. Kawakami, L., Knabben, A., Rechia, D., Bastos, D., Pereira,O., Silva, R., Santos, L.: A test automation framework for mobile phones. In: Proceedings of the 8th IEEE Latin American Test Workshop. IEEE Computer Society (2007)
9. Kiczales, G., Lamping, J., Mendhekar, A., Maeda, C., Lopes, C., Loingtier, J.-M., Irwin, J.: Aspect-oriented programming. In: Proceedings of European Conference on Object-Oriented Programming (ECOOP), Lecture Notes in Computer Science, pp. 220–242 (1997)
10. Leavens, G.T., Baker, A.L., Ruby, C.: Preliminary design of JML: a behavioral interface specification language for Java. SIGSOFT Softw. Eng. Not. **31**(3), 1–38 (2006)
11. Nielson, F., Nielson, H.R., Hankin, C.: Principles of Program Analysis. Springer, New York (1999)
12. Parnas, D.L.: On the criteria to be used in decomposing systems into modules. CACM **15**(12), 1053–1058 (1972)
13. Ribeiro, M., Borba, P., Kästner, C.: Feature maintenance with emergent interfaces. In: Proceedings of the International Conference on Software Engineering (ICSE), pp. 989–1000. ACM (2014)
14. Ribeiro, M., Borba, P.: Towards feature modularization. In: Doctoral Symposium of the International Conference on Object-Oriented Programming Systems Languages and Applications (OOPSLA), pp. 225–226. ACM (2010)
15. Ribeiro, M., Pacheco, H., Teixeira, L., Borba, P.: Emergent feature modularization. In: Onward!, Affiliated with International Conference on Systems, Programming, Languages and Applications: Software for Humanity (SPLASH), pp. 11–18. ACM (2010)
16. Ribeiro, M., Toledo, T., Borba, P., Brabrand, C.: A tool for improving maintainabiliy of preprocessor-based product lines. In: Tools Session of the 2nd Brazilian Congress on Software (CBSoft) (2011)
17. Ribeiro, M., Toledo, T., Winther, J., Brabrand, C., Borba, P.: Emergo: a tool for improving maintainabiliy of preprocessor-based product lines. In: Proceedings of the 11th International Conference on Aspect-Oriented Software Development (AOSD), Companion, Demo Track, pp. 23–26. ACM (2012)
18. Winther, J.: Experimental Java compiler, January 2012. http://users-cs.au.dk/jwbrics/java

Chapter 5
Evaluation

Abstract In this chapter we present the evaluation of our work. In particular, we investigate and compare maintenance effort when maintaining features with and without Emergent Interfaces. Then, we evaluate the performance of the brute-force analysis when compared to both feature-sensitive analyses we present in this book. Investigating and pointing out the fastest plays an important role on deciding which one we should use in our tool.

Keywords GQM · Empirical studies · Virtual separation of concerns · Maintenance effort · Performance

5.1 General Setting: Goal, Questions, and Metrics

To better structure our evaluation, we use the Goal, Questions, and Metrics (GQM) [1] approach. Our evaluation aims to compare (i) maintenance effort with and without Emergent Interfaces during maintenance tasks involving features implemented with preprocessors [9] as well as (ii) the performance of the brute-force analysis and our feature-sensitive analyses [2].

Regarding the effort evaluation, we consider the hiding facilities (VSoC) because it provides benefits when compared to `#ifdefs` [6]. Basically, it improves comprehensibility, separation of concerns, and avoids subtle errors by only allowing disciplined annotations.

In particular, we investigate the following questions:

- **Question 1**: Do Emergent Interfaces reduce effort during maintenance tasks involving feature code dependencies in preprocessor-based systems?[1]
- **Question 2**: When considering the brute-force analysis and our two feature-sensitive analyses, which one is the fastest?

---

[1] Here, software families and product lines that use preprocessors to implement feature code.

© The Author(s) 2014
M. Ribeiro et al., *Emergent Interfaces for Feature Modularization*,
SpringerBriefs in Computer Science, DOI 10.1007/978-3-319-11493-4_5

Fig. 5.1 Maintaining the
`screen` variable

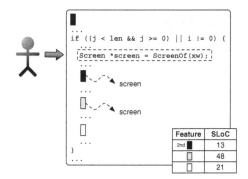

Now we present the metrics to answer these questions. To answer **Question 1**,
we use the following metrics:

- Source Lines of Code (*SLoC*) to analyze during a maintenance task;
- Number of Fragments (*NoFa*) to analyze during a maintenance task;
- Number of Features (*NoFe*) to analyze during a maintenance task.

To better explain the metrics we use in this book, consider the code snippet from
xterm illustrated in Fig. 5.1. In this particular example, we have four hidden code
fragments—we denote by *fragment* any preprocessor directive such as `#ifdef`,
`#else`, `#elif`, and so forth—which consist of three features (*black*, *gray*, and
white). The developer should maintain the `screen` variable (changing its type,
changing the parameter `xw`, etc.). Notice that there is a fragment outside the `screen`
scope. Therefore, when maintaining such a variable, the developer does not need to
analyze that fragment (see the fragment on the top of Fig. 5.1).

To perform this maintenance, the developer needs to open and analyze each fragment to be sure that the maintenance she performs does not impact them. If she
analyzes three fragments (features *black*, *gray*, and *white*), we have the following
values for the metrics: *NoFa* = 3, *NoFe* = 3, and *SLoC* = 82 (13 + 48 + 21). This is
a typical case of not using Emergent Interfaces. She has no information about dependencies, forcing her to open and analyze all fragments. Notice that, for this particular
maintenance task, we ignore the fragment outside the `screen` scope from our cal-
culations. On the other hand, if she analyzes only the *black* and *gray* fragments,
we have *NoFa* = 2, *NoFe* = 2, and *SLoC* = 61 (13 + 48). Here she analyzes the
fragments that indeed use the `screen` variable. This would be the case of using
Emergent Interfaces.

To answer **Question 2**, we use the following metric:

- *Time* to execute in all methods of a preprocessor-based system the brute force
  reaching definitions analysis and the lifted (consecutive and simultaneous) reaching definitions analysis.

To summarize, we split our evaluation into two parts. As mentioned, the first
one consists of an effort study (Sect. 5.2) to measure maintenance effort using the

Fig. 5.2 Goal, Questions, and Metrics perspective

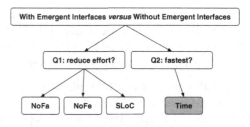

following proxy metrics [7, 8]: *NoFa, NoFe*, and *SLoC*. To measure the performance of the brute-force analysis and our feature-sensitive analyses, we use the *Time* metric. Figure 5.2 summarizes our Goal, Question, and Metrics perspective. The white leaf boxes represent the metrics we use in our effort study. The gray one represents the metric for the performance study.

To investigate **Question 1**, we use 43 preprocessor-based software families and product lines of different domains, sizes, and languages (C and Java). We list them in Table 3.1 (Chap. 3). Notice that they range from simple systems to complex ones such as linux. The majority is written in C and all of them contain several features implemented using preprocessor directives. To answer **Question 2**, we use four qualitatively different product lines: *GPL, MobileMedia, Lampiro*, and *BerkeleyDB*. They have very different numbers in terms of SLoC, number of methods, and number of features.

5.2 Effort Study

In this section we present our effort study to answer **Question 1**.

5.2.1 Study Setting

To perform an empirical study on maintenance effort, we first need to identify feature code dependencies. Chapter 3 presents data with respect to how often features dependencies (*MDe*) occur in the 43 families and product lines we consider. We also present the feature code dependencies we consider in Fig. 3.5. So, given these feature dependencies we compute, we evaluate *how* they impact on maintenance effort with and without Emergent Interfaces.

In this empirical study, we estimate maintenance effort by means of the number of source lines of code (*SLoC*), fragments (*NoFa*), and features (*NoFe*) we should analyze during a maintenance task. Therefore, the higher these metrics, the greater the maintenance effort. Notice that we can observe the same effort regardless of the approach (with or without Emergent Interfaces). This happens when our technique points out feature dependencies in all fragments we indeed have to analyze. In this context, Emergent interfaces reduce the effort when at least one fragment does not have dependencies with the feature we are maintaining.

To evaluate effort, in this study we have the following assumptions:

1. With Emergent Interfaces, developers would open and analyze only the fragments pointed by the interface;
2. Without Emergent Interfaces, developers would open and analyze all fragments within the method, since at first she does not know in which fragments there are feature dependencies.

To perform this effort study, we randomly select methods with feature dependencies and then compute the proxy metrics for each approach (with or without Emergent Interfaces). To have a representative study, we now need to tackle the problem of *which* methods we should select to perform the evaluation. On the one hand, if we select only methods with many fragments, we are favoring Emergent Interfaces, since the probability of finding at least one fragment with no feature dependency increases. On the other hand, if we select only methods with few fragments (one for instance), we are not able show differences between both approaches since the effort would often be the same. Hence, we need to select the methods carefully. To guarantee the selection of methods with both characteristics and then provide a better representative study, we consider the following two groups:

- **Group 1**: methods with 1 or 2 fragments; and
- **Group 2**: methods with more than 2 fragments.

Notice we chose 2 as our threshold (to divide our groups) because the differences between both approaches become visible when a developer has to examine at least two fragments. In methods with feature dependencies, both approaches always have the same effort when we have only one fragment (same $SLoC$, $NoFa = 1$, and $NoFe = 1$).

Now that we have the groups defined, we randomly select methods accordingly. Firstly, we decided to pick three methods per family and per product line. Since methods of **Group 1** are more common, we would have two methods of **Group 1** and only one of **Group 2**. However, depending on the family and product line, the quantity of methods of both groups varies significantly. For example, when considering the *libxml2*, we have 953 methods in **Group 1** and 125 methods in **Group 2**. So, we rather select the methods proportionally according to each family and product line (instead of three methods for all). In this way, for *libxml2*, we select eight method of **Group 1** and one of **Group 2**. Because we compute the metrics manually, the lower threshold is the minimum, 1. Therefore, we select only one method from the group that contains less methods. The upper threshold is the number of methods of the group that contains more methods divided by the number of methods of the other group.

In this way, our idea consists of selecting methods with feature dependencies to fit both groups proportionally according to each family and product line. Because a method may have more than one variable with dependencies, we also randomly

Table 5.1 Number of families/SPLs with their respective methods proportions

Number of families/SPLs	Group 1	Group 2
23	1	1
13	2	1
3 (gimp, gnumeric, lampiro)	3	1
2 (parrot, linux)	4	1
1 (libxml2)	8	1
1 (sendmail)	1	5

select one variable per method. Then, we begin our effort evaluation from that variable taking its scope into consideration. Notice that we simulate a developer supposed to change a single variable. Remove the variable declaration, change its value, and change its type are examples of tasks a developer may perform. From this variable, we manually compute the three metrics to estimate the maintenance effort.

Finally, we consider three replications. Our idea consists of repeating the entire effort evaluation three times so we can take the average of three independent observations.

We summarize how we perform our evaluation as an algorithm (see Algorithm 1).

Algorithm 1 General algorithm of our effort estimation study.

---
while we do not reach 3 replications **do**
  for each family/SPL **do**
    - Randomly select methods with feature dependencies proportionally to fit the groups;
    for each method **do**
      - Randomly select a variable;
      - From this variable, compute the effort ($SLoC$, $NoFa$, and $NoFe$) with and without Emergent
       Interfaces.
    end for
  end for
end while

5.2.2 Results and Discussion

We evaluate effort with three replications. For each replication, we randomly select 122 methods from all families and product lines. We select all methods proportionally according to each particular family and product line to fit the two groups. Table 5.1 shows the number of families and product lines with their respective method proportions according to each group. For instance, in *parrot* and *linux* we select four methods of **Group 1** and one of **Group 2**. Only the *sendmail* software family has more methods of **Group 2**. Notice that this is consistent with our previous claim that methods of **Group 1** are more common.

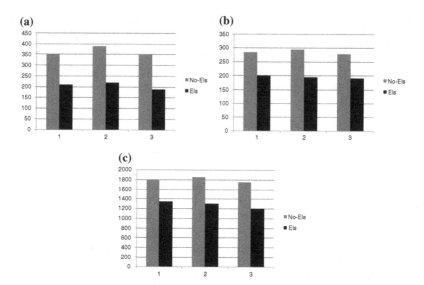

Fig. 5.3 Fragments, features and *SLoC* that developers should analyze in the selected methods with and without Emergent Interfaces. **a** Fragments. **b** Features. **c** SLoC

As discussed, to estimate maintenance effort, we consider three proxy metrics: *SLoC*, *NoFa*, and *NoFe*. We show the results for each replication and each metric in Fig. 5.3. Each bar summarizes one particular metric for all 122 methods we selected. The idea consists of summarizing the effort of both approaches (with and without Emergent Interfaces) and then compare them. Notice that Emergent Interfaces reduce the effort in all replications and metrics. When considering the average of the three replications, with Emergent Interfaces, developers would analyze 35 % less fragments; 25 % less features; and 35 % less source lines of code.

Actually, we already expected that the effort reduction for features would be smaller when compared to the fragments reduction. Based on the interface information, when developers discard fragments from their analyses to achieve a given maintenance task, they also discard *SLoC*. However, this is not true for features, since we might have two fragments of the same feature, which means that discarding one fragment does not necessarily mean discarding the whole feature from the analysis.

Regarding the number of methods, developers have less effort in 33 % of methods for replication 1, in 34 % for replication 2, and in 39 % of methods for replication 3. Nevertheless, this result is not interesting when analyzed in isolation. But when we cross these numbers with the number of families and product lines we achieve maintenance effort gains, we observe that these methods are scattered throughout the majority of the families and product lines we study. This may be an indicator that Emergent Interfaces might reduce effort in different situations such as different domains, sizes, languages, etc. Table 5.2 shows, for each replication, the number of

Table 5.2   Total of methods and families/SPLs where emergent interfaces reduced effort

Replication	Methods (less effort)	Families/SPLs (less effort)
1	40 (33%)	34 (79%)
2	41 (34%)	36 (84%)
3	47 (39%)	36 (84%)

Table 5.3   Distribution of methods into their groups

Methods (less effort)	Group 1	Group 2
40 (33%)	7	33
41 (34%)	7	34
47 (39%)	14	33

families and product lines where Emergent Interfaces reduce the effort in at least one method.

Table 5.2 shows the total of methods in which Emergent Interfaces reduce maintenance effort. Table 5.3 distributes these methods into the respective groups they belong to. As illustrated, the majority of the methods where Emergent Interfaces reduce effort belongs to **Group 2** (i.e., the one where methods have more than 2 fragments).

Previously, we discussed we could favor our interfaces in case of selecting only methods with many fragments (methods of **Group 2**). We believe that this hypothesis is true because when the *NoFa* increases, the probability of finding at least one fragment with no feature dependency increases as well. In this case, the maintenance effort is smaller with Emergent Interfaces. The results we present in Table 5.3 suggest that our claim might be true.

Nevertheless, to further support this claim, we analyze the methods of **Group 2** more deeply. This group has 47 methods with more than 2 fragments for all replications. According to our results (see Table 5.3), Emergent Interfaces reduce effort in 33, 34, and 33 methods for each replication. Therefore, we achieve effort reduction in 70, 72, and 70 % of the methods of this group. Figure 5.4 illustrates that, in general, when the number of fragments increases, the percentage of methods in which we achieve maintenance effort reduction also increases. For instance, if we take only methods with more than 4 fragments into account, we have effort reduction in 83, 82 and 84 % of those methods.

According to our results, Emergent Interfaces achieve effort reduction in $35.25 \pm 3.6\%$ of the randomly selected methods. The reduction happens in $82 \pm 2.7\%$ of the families and product lines we analyzed. Thus, our results suggest that our interfaces may reduce effort regarding the simple maintenance activities we focus here, like when changing the value of a variable.

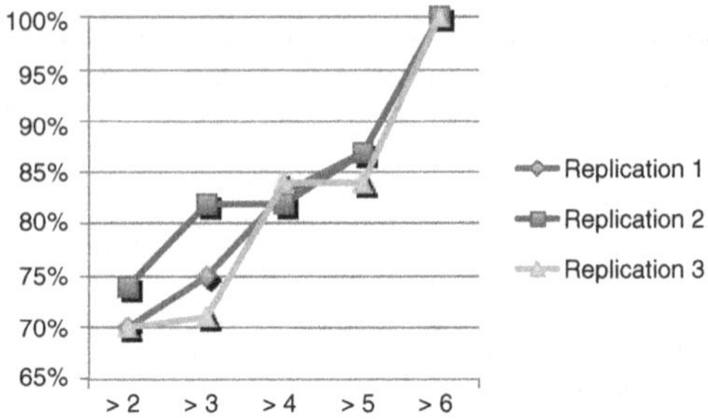

Fig. 5.4 Estimating maintenance effort reduction when increasing the number of fragments

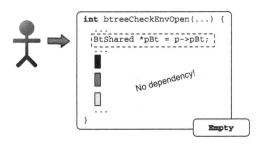

Fig. 5.5 Variable with no feature dependency

5.2.3 Answering Question 1

Next we answer **Question 1** based on our effort study. **Question 1** is the following: *Do Emergent Interfaces reduce effort during maintenance tasks involving feature code dependencies in preprocessor-based systems?*

Without Emergent Interfaces, developers do not have any information about the existence or absence of feature dependencies, so they need to check this in the existing fragments. If we have many of them, the effort clearly increases. However, notice that in 64.75 % of the methods we analyze, the effort estimation is the same: *NoFa*, *NoFe*, and *SLoC* have the same values regardless of Emergent Interfaces. Thus, the negative impact on maintenance effort without Emergent Interfaces seems to be not so common.

Based on our study, we can conclude that Emergent Interfaces reduce maintenance effort. We observe more significant gains achieved by our technique in methods with many fragments. However, only 38 % of the methods belong to **Group 2**, which means that methods with many fragments occur occasionally. Nevertheless, although we neither evaluated nor focused on methods without dependencies, Emergent Interfaces also provide benefits in these cases. For example, Fig. 5.5 illustrates a method from *BerkeleyDB*. The developer should change the pBt value. No feature uses this variable. Notice that when there is no dependency, the Emergent Interface is empty, so there is no need to check any fragment. In contrast, without Emergent Interfaces developers do not have this information, which may lead them to analyze unnecessary code (all three features).

5.2.4 Threats to Validity

Now, we present the threats to validity of our effort study.

5.2.4.1 Conclusion Validity

The proxy metrics [8] we use are not sufficient to measure directly how much the maintenance effort reduces. Instead, our metrics can estimate effort (actually, time to accomplish a maintenance task is a better metric to measure effort). However, they are able to show differences with and without Emergent Interfaces. Although not sufficient, the metrics are still useful to better understand the benefits promoted by Emergent Interfaces.

5.2.4.2 Internal Validity

We do not take feature models into consideration, so the results of our metrics may change due to feature constraints we are not aware of. Nevertheless, we believe that this changes our effort results only slightly, because the majority of methods we use in our evaluation belongs to **Group 1** (methods with 1 or 2 fragments). However, we can only have constraints with 2 different features or more.

5.2.4.3 External Validity

The notion of dependency we consider in this effort study is a limitation. Our script tool computes only *simple dependencies*, as showed in Fig. 3.6a. However, there are more dependencies neglected by our study, such as *chain of assignments* (Fig. 3.6b) and *interprocedural* (Fig. 3.6c). Since both kinds of dependencies are not present in our statistics, we believe that the real number of dependencies we present to answer **Question 1** is even higher. In this context, there is a risk when raising the number of dependencies: if one has to analyze all fragments, using or not Emergent Interfaces seems meaningless. In cases where there are feature dependencies in all fragments,[2] we still have some benefits: tools that compute and generate Emergent Interfaces can point exactly (the lines of code) where the dependencies are. Therefore, instead of analyzing a fragment with lots of lines of code, developers can focus on particular lines of code that indeed contain dependencies.

---

[2] Based on our experience when analyzing preprocessor-based families and product lines, although this case might happen within a method, this situation does not hold for *interprocedural* dependencies.

Table 5.4 Various size metrics for our four software product line benchmarks

Benchmark	SLoC	$|\mathbb{F}_{global}|$	$|2^{\mathbb{F}_{local}}|$	#methods	#ifdef (%)
GPL	1,350	18	$2^9 = 512$	135 (964)	82
MobileMedia	5,700	14	$2^7 = 128$	285 (821)	45
Lampiro	45,000	11	$2^2 = 4$	1,949 (1,980)	1.5
BerkeleyDB	84,000	42	$2^7 = 128$	3,605 (7,446)	40

5.3 Performance

In this section we present an evaluation in terms of performance. In particular, we investigate the performance of our feature-sensitive approaches. Since interactive tools like Emergo should be able to quickly respond to developers actions, our evaluation is important to consider the fastest approach in our emergent tool. This section intends to answer **Question 2**.

5.3.1 Study Setting

To validate our feature-sensitive approaches, we have implemented and used the reaching definitions *intraprocedural* dataflow analysis using the SOOT framework [3, 10] for analyzing Java programs.[3] We have subsequently lifted this analysis into consecutive and simultaneous feature-sensitive analyses as presented in Sect. 4.4. Because we are using *intraprocedural* analyses which analyze one method at a time, we use the *local* set of configurations, $\mathbb{F}_{local}$, local to each method. This significantly reduces the size of the lattices we work with. However, instead of using the set of valid configurations, we use the set of all feature combinations, $2^{\mathbb{F}_{local}}$. Restricting to valid configurations only would make both feature-sensitive analyses faster.

In terms of benchmarks, we have four qualitatively different product lines annotated using colors with the CIDE support, summarized in Fig. 5.4. We use only the following four benchmarks because our SOOT implementation relies on product lines annotated with colors. *GPL* is a product line of desktop applications of small size with intensive feature usage [5]. *MobileMedia* is a product line of mobile applications for dealing with multi-media of small size and moderate feature usage [4]. *Lampiro* is a product line of instant-messaging clients with low feature usage. Finally, *BerkeleyDB* is a product line of databases [5].

Table 5.4 summarizes SLoC; $|\mathbb{F}_{global}|$, as the total number of features in the SPL; $|2^{\mathbb{F}_{local}}|$, as the maximum number of configurations of any one method in the product line; #methods, as the number of methods with the total number of different method

---

[3] As we illustrate in this section, we evaluate our feature-sensitive approaches using SOOT. But since the implementation of *interprocedural* analyses using this framework is not straightforward, we decide to use another framework to implement Emergo.

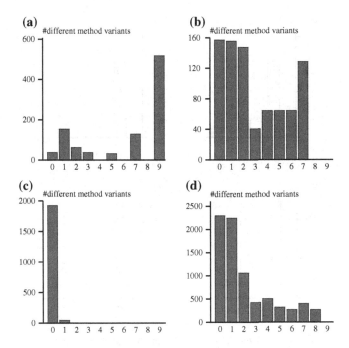

Fig. 5.6 Histogram showing the distribution of number of configurations per methods. **a** GPL. **b** MobileMedia. **c** Lampiro. **d** BerkeleyDB

variants in parentheses; and "#ifdef %", as the percentage of methods with feature usage.

Figure 5.6 illustrates the distribution of the number of configurations per method for each product line. *MobileMedia* (depicted in Fig. 5.6b), for example, has 157 methods without features, 78 methods with one feature (i.e., $2^1 * 78 = 156$ different end-product methods), 37 methods with two features (i.e., $2^2 * 37 = 148$ different method variants), ..., and one method with seven features (i.e., $2^7 * 1 = 128$ different method variants). The area illustrated in the histograms is therefore directly proportional to the number of method variants. This way, Fig. 5.6 shows that the four benchmarks have qualitatively different feature usage profiles.

5.3.2 Results and Discussion

Figure 5.7 plots the total time for the reaching definitions analysis on each of our four benchmarks running on a 64-bit machine with a Intel ® Core™ i7 920 CPU running at a 2.6 GHz frequency with 8 GB of memory on a Linux Ubuntu 2.6.32-30-generic operating system. All times given are averages over ten runs with the highest and lowest numbers removed.

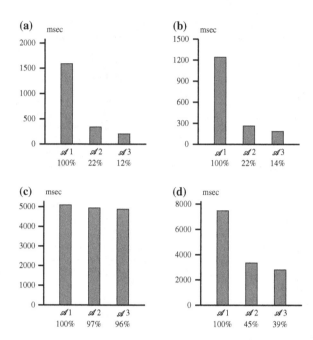

Fig. 5.7 The total time of *reaching definitions* for all configurations using $\mathscr{A}$1 versus $\mathscr{A}$2 versus $\mathscr{A}$3. $\mathscr{A}$1 consists of *jimplification* + *analysis*; $\mathscr{A}$2 and $\mathscr{A}$3 consist of *jimplification* + *CFG instrumentation* + *analysis*. **a** GPL. **b** MobileMedia. **c** Lampiro. **d** BerkeleyDB

For the feature-oblivious brute force analysis, $\mathscr{A}$1, the time includes *jimplification* (compilation from Java to Jimple, an intermediate program representation used by SOOT) and the *analysis* (fixed-point computation) for the reaching definitions analysis, but excluding *preprocessing* (resolving the #ifdef directives) which is negligent. The jimplification time given is the average compilation time of the *slowest* configuration to compile ($c = 2^{\mathbb{F}}$) and the *fastest* configuration to compile ($c = \emptyset$) times the number of configurations to be compiled. We have to do this estimation because several configurations, although valid, generate code that does not compile.

For the feature-sensitive analyses, $\mathscr{A}$2 and $\mathscr{A}$3, the time comprises *jimplification*, *CFG instrumentation*, and *analysis*.

As can be seen, the feature-sensitive analyses, $\mathscr{A}$2 and $\mathscr{A}$3, are faster than the brute-force approach, $\mathscr{A}$1, on all benchmarks except on *Lampiro* where they are all fairly equal. Further, $\mathscr{A}$3 is faster than $\mathscr{A}$2. When compared to $\mathscr{A}$1, $\mathscr{A}$3 does the same analysis but takes only 12% of the time on *GPL*, 14% on *MobileMedia*, 96% on *Lampiro*, and 39% on *BerkeleyDB* which translates into a gain factors of respectively: 8.1, 6.9, 1.0, and 2.6. In other words, $\mathscr{A}$3 is anywhere from slightly to slightly more than eight times faster than $\mathscr{A}$1.

For $\mathscr{A}$1, the time of jimplification for all the benchmarks dominates that of the analysis, except for *Lampiro*. When considering $\mathscr{A}$2 and $\mathscr{A}$3, the jimplification time is a constant overhead we only have to pay once even if we perform many analyses.

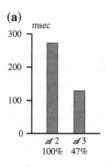

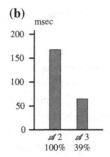

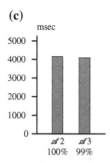

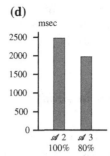

Fig. 5.8 The analysis time of *reaching definitions* using $\mathscr{A}2$ vs. $\mathscr{A}3$. **a** GPL. **b** MobileMedia. **c** Lampiro. **d** BerkeleyDB

Thus, we now focus more on the time of the analyses, disregarding jimplification time.

Figure 5.8 plots the relative difference between the speed of the consecutive and simultaneous feature-sensitive analyses using the reaching definitions analysis. We observe that the simultaneous analysis $\mathscr{A}3$ is faster on all the benchmarks, although only slightly so on *Lampiro*. When compared to $\mathscr{A}2$, it spends only 47 % of the time on *GPL*, 39 % on *MobileMedia*, 99 % on *Lampiro*, and 80 % on *BerkeleyDB*.

It is not surprising that the analysis time is almost the same for *Lampiro*. This happens because it has so limited feature usage (only 1.5 % of the methods have features), that most of the cost is the time of the analysis itself without any overhead from features. In fact, the analysis time for *Lampiro* is virtually the same for all three analyses. We take this as indication that the overhead of our approach is almost nothing for product lines with low feature usage. Also, it does not matter much which of the two feature-sensitive analyses are used in such cases.

5.3.3 Answering Question 2

Next we answer **Question 2**, which is the following: *When considering the brute-force analysis and our two feature-sensitive analyses, which one is the fastest?*

Based on our performance study, we have evidence that the simultaneous feature-sensitive analysis, $\mathscr{A}3$, seems to be the fastest. If we average the speed ratio over the two analyses on the four product lines, $\mathscr{A}3$ outperforms $\mathscr{A}2$ in using only about 60 % of the time to calculate the same information. We believe that $\mathscr{A}3$ is faster because it only has to do one fixed-point computation instead of one per configuration. However, it is important to note that $\mathscr{A}3$ will have a larger memory footprint when compared to $\mathscr{A}2$. This happens because it has to keep all configurations in memory during the fixed-point computation (which can be exponentially more than $\mathscr{A}2$). This, however, does not seem to be a problem in this *intraprocedural* analysis as it only analyses one method at a time. Indeed, we have not been able to notice this problem on the four benchmarks used.

5.3.4 Threats to Validity

Regarding conclusion to validity, we do not execute statistical tests to analyze the statistic significance of the time differences. Therefore, we see differences in our Barplots but they actually might not exist.

Regarding external validity, we use only four benchmarks. However, we believe our results should hold for other ones, because we take four qualitatively different product lines. They range from simple toy ones to complex and real ones. In addition, all have different feature usage.

References

1. Basili, V.R., Caldiera, G., Dieter Rombach, H., The goal question metric approach. In: Encyclopedia of Software Engineering. Wiley (1994)
2. Brabrand, C., Ribeiro, M., Tolêdo, T., Borba, P., Intraprocedural dataflow analysis for software product lines. In: Proceedings of the 11th International Conference on Aspect-Oriented Software Development (AOSD), pp. 13–24. ACM (2012)
3. Einarsson, Á., Nielsen, J.D.: A survivor's guide to Java program analysis with soot. http://www.brics.dk/SootGuide/ (2008)
4. Figueiredo, E., Cacho, N., Sant'Anna, C., Monteiro, M., Kulesza, U., Garcia, A., Soares, S., Ferrari, F., Khan, S., Filho, F., Dantas, F.: Evolving software product lines with aspects: an empirical study on design stability. In: Proceedings of the 30th International Conference on Software Engineering (ICSE), pp. 261–270. ACM (2008)
5. Kästner, C., Apel, S., Kuhlemann, M.: Granularity in software product lines. In: Proceedings of the 30th International Conference on Software Engineering (ICSE), pp. 311–320. ACM (2008)
6. Kästner, C., Apel, S.: Virtual separation of concerns—a second chance for preprocessors. J. Object Technol. **8**(6), 59–78 (2009)

7. Keeney, R.L., Gregory, R.S.: Selecting attributes to measure the achievement of objectives. Oper. Res. **53**(1), 1–11 (2005)
8. Kyle McKay, S., Pruitt, B.A., Harberg, M., Covich, A.P., Kenney, M.A., Craig Fischenich, J.: Metric development for environmental benefits analysis. Technical Report ERDC TN-EMRRP-EBA-4 (2010)
9. Ribeiro, M., Queiroz, F., Borba, P., Tolêdo, T., Brabrand, C., Soares, S.: On the impact of feature dependencies when maintaining preprocessor-based software product lines. In: Proceedings of the 10th International Conference on Generative Programming and Component Engineering (GPCE), pp. 23–32. ACM (2011)
10. Soot: a Java Optimization Framework. http://www.sable.mcgill.ca/soot/ (2010)

Chapter 6
Comparison with Other Approaches

Abstract In this chapter we discuss several previous work on topics like interfaces for non-annotative approaches (such as aspect-oriented programming), separation of concerns and modularity, analyses on preprocessor-based systems, and dataflow analysis. Besides discussing, we compare these works to our approach, pointing out the differences between them.

Keywords Interfaces · Separation of concerns · Preprocessors · Dataflow analysis · Safe composition · Maintainability

6.1 Interfaces for Non-annotative Approaches

In this work, we focus on interfaces for techniques that annotate the source code to define feature boundaries, such as conditional compilation. Because this leads to feature scattering and tangling, we and others [2–5, 9, 29–31] applied and evaluated the use of AOP (Aspect-Oriented Programming) to solve these problems. However, because of problems like fragile pointcuts [32], interfaces between classes and aspects were proposed in order to achieve modularity.

Griswold et al. [15] proposed interfaces for aspect-based systems named Crosscutting Programming Interfaces (XPIs). XPIs consist of abstract interfaces aiming at decoupling the aspects from details of classes, providing better modularity during parallel maintenance. In addition, XPIs rely on the notion of provides and requires that may be checked by such interfaces. For instance, we might define a contract in which aspects cannot change the state of some object. To write a XPI, developers might use AspectJ [21, 24] language constructs. In this way, components and interfaces have a rigid structure: they are classes, aspects, and XPIs (written as aspects as well). Unlike XPIs, our approach does not predefine components and interfaces. They emerge on demand, according to a given maintenance task. Besides, we do not write Emergent Interfaces. Thus, they do not need language constructs. Rather, our interfaces depend on tools, which are responsible for generating them. Like XPIs, our interfaces abstract details of features, being important to make developers focus on the maintenance task.

© The Author(s) 2014
M. Ribeiro et al., *Emergent Interfaces for Feature Modularization*,
SpringerBriefs in Computer Science, DOI 10.1007/978-3-319-11493-4_6

Open Modules [1] propose the use of interfaces for exposing join points in classes, limiting the scope of advised code to the join points exposed by the class developer. Although join point hiding is an important concern, it does not provide information to the aspect developer (beyond exported join points) that could be useful for establishing contracts that serve as interfaces between OO and AO developers. Open modules require language constructs, whereas our Emergent Interfaces need tool support.

The AspectScope tool [16] is a programming tool that realizes the idea of aspect-aware interfaces in AspectJ [20]. It performs whole-program analysis of AspectJ programs and displays module interfaces according to current deployment of aspects. AspectScope aims to guide developers on understanding the program behavior with local reasoning. Their concept of presenting interfaces to the developer is similar to what we propose, which aims to facilitate modular reasoning through tool support. However, AspectScope module interfaces are not feature aware and focus only on aspects.

6.2 Separation of Concerns

Some approaches provide separation of concerns by hiding information. Mylyn [19] is a task-focused approach to reduce information overload, so that only artifacts (like packages, classes, and methods) relevant to a current task are visible. This information is filtered by using a task context that is created during a programming activity. This way, tasks are monitored by Mylyn aiming at storing information about what developers are doing in order to complete the task. If the task is not completed, developers can continue them afterwards. When opening the IDE to complete that task, instead of showing thousands of artifacts, developers select the task and Mylyn provides only the artifacts related to it, improving productivity and reducing the information overload. Notice that developers do not spend time searching for the artifacts of that task. Like Mylyn, our approach also needs a selection. The developer selects the snippet to maintain, whereas when using Mylyn developers select tasks. Our interfaces and the task context of Mylyn emerge during maintenance. Last but not least, we also provide information reduction, since only elements shared with other features are showed to the developer responsible for the *Selection* component.

Colored IDE (CIDE) is an Eclipse-based tool for decomposing legacy applications into features [17]. Although CIDE uses the preprocessors semantics (it is based on the same annotative approach), it avoids pollution of code, which means that `#ifdef` directives are no longer needed. Instead, it relies on the Eclipse editor to define the features boundaries through background colors. CIDE relies on the VSoC approach, which means that it is possible to hide features code not relevant to the current maintenance task. CIDE also has a product-line-aware type checking that catches errors. Differently, our intent is to use Emergent Interfaces to *prevent* errors like these and going further by also preventing behavior errors.

Conceptual Module [7] is an approach to support developers on maintenance tasks. They set lines of code to be part of a conceptual module. Then, developers use queries to capture other lines that should be part of that conceptual module and to compute dependencies among other conceptual modules. Similarly, we also catch dependencies, but we go beyond by considering features relationships. Both approaches abstract details from developers. This way, during maintenance activities, they concentrate on relationships among features or conceptual modules rather than on code of no interest, being important for comprehensibility.

6.3 Safe Composition

Safe composition is related to safe generation and the verification of properties for product lines assets. It provides guarantees that the product derivation process generates products with particular properties that are obeyed [12, 18, 33]. Due to the potential complexity of SPLs, this problem might be difficult to check manually, and generating all SPL products turns out to be impractical as the SPL becomes larger.

Thaker et al. present techniques for verifying type safety properties of AHEAD [8] product lines using FMs and SAT solvers [33]. Properties are extracted from feature modules and verified that they hold for all product line members. Delaware et al. extends this work, proving soundness of the underlying type system [12].

Kstner et al. propose safe composition for the Color Featherweight Java (CFJ) calculus [18]. This calculus established type rules to ensure that only well-typed programs can be generated. They formally prove that—given a well-typed CFJ SPL— all possible variants that can be generated are well-typed FJ programs, i.e., generation preserves typing. This formalization is implemented in CIDE, to check type-safety of Java SPLs annotated with colors.

These works focus on product-line-aware type systems, that is, they check for type errors for all SPL variants. We can catch some of these typing errors. However, our intent is to use Emergent Interfaces to prevent errors when maintaining a feature. Besides, some elements in our interfaces are concerned with the system behaviour (assignment of values), rather than only with static type information.

6.4 Analyses on Preprocessor-Based Systems

Some researches assess the way developers use preprocessors in product lines. Recently, researchers [27] created and computed many metrics to analyze, for instance, the feature code scattering and tangling when using conditional compilation directives. To do so, they analyzed 40 families and product lines implemented in C. They formulated research questions and answered them with the aid of a tool, which is able to compute the metrics. We complement this work by taking feature dependencies into account. We extend the tool provided by these researchers so we can compute metrics like *number of methods with feature dependencies* (*MDe*). We also complement this work with respect to different product lines (the ones written in Java).

Researchers [28] studied the use of preprocessor-based code in several systems written in C. `#ifdefs` directives are indeed powerful, so programmers can make all kinds of annotations using them. Consequently, developers can introduce subtle errors like annotating a closing bracket but not the opening one. They call this kind of annotation "undisciplined". On the other hand, disciplined annotations hold properties that are useful for preprocessor-aware parsing tools so we can represent annotations as nodes in the AST. Wrapping entirely functions and statements are examples of disciplined annotations. In their study, they found that the majority of the preprocessor directives usage are disciplined (84.4 %). We also complement this work, but we focus on feature dependencies and consider different product lines and metrics in our evaluation.

Another study regarding preprocessor usage [13] concludes that, despite their evident shortcomings, the controlled use of preprocessors can improve portability, performance, or even readability. They found that most systems analyzed in their studies make heavy use of preprocessor directives. Similarly to our work, they compute the occurrence of conditional compilation directives. Differently, we did not find a lot of preprocessor usage like they did. However, notice we focus only on methods with conditional compilation directives. In contrast, they focus on the entire code (not only methods) and analyze many other kinds of preprocessors, such as macros.

Recently, researchers have shown in a series of controlled experiments that different representations of preprocessor annotations can improve program comprehension [14]. In addition, another study have shown in a controlled experiment that hiding irrelevant code fragments can improve understanding of product lines [26]. These results complement each other and help building a tool environment for efficient maintenance of preprocessor-based implementations.

A recent work [11] discusses that it is essential to investigate if research results obtained from small product lines can be extrapolated to complex ones. To minimize the problem of unavailability of public and realistic product lines, they provide an experiment in which they extract features from ArgoUML [6], an open source tool widely used to design UML diagrams. In particular, they extracted 8 features, that together correspond to 31 % of the entire ArgoUML code. To do so, they used preprocessors and computed metrics with respect to size, crosscutting nature, granularity, and localization. We do not perform any feature extraction. Instead, we complement recent studies [27, 28] by providing data on preprocessor usage.

6.5 Dataflow Analysis for Maintainability

We can compute our Emergent Interfaces by using a so-called slicing [36]. A program slice consists of the program parts that potentially affect the values computed at some point of interest. We can also see program slice in the forward direction, where we define a point and the slice consists of the program parts that are potentially affected by such a point [34]. Our idea fits in forward static slicing based on data, where we define the points of interest (our maintenance points) and then interfaces with respect to other parts of the program emerge. In contrast, we take feature relationships into account.

Researchers [25] observed developers facing problems of understanding code during several maintenance tasks. They found that a significant amount of a developer's work involves answering "reachability questions". A reachability question is a search across the code for statements that match a given search criteria. In addition, they observe that developers often insert defects because they did not answer the reachability question successfully. In our context, we could search for feature dependencies. If we cannot answer where they are or which features (or feature combinations) they belong to, we can introduce errors. A reachability question consists of expressing a query about statements. IDE standard tools might help on answering reachability questions but they are not feature sensitive.

Testing SPLs is hard as it may require examination of many products. However, there are features whose presence or absence do not influence some of the test outcomes, which makes many feature combinations unnecessary for a particular test, reducing the effort when testing SPL and increasing productivity. This idea of selecting only relevant features for a given test case was proposed in a recent work [22]. The work uses dataflow analysis to recover a list of features that are reachable from a given test case. Because the analysis yields only reachable features, the other ones are discarded, decreasing the number of combinations to be tested. Afterwards, the reachable features as well as the feature model are used to discover which combinations should be tested. In some sense, the dataflow analysis considers features (the reachable ones). But it is not completely feature sensitive, since feature model information is not used during the analysis. In contrast, we defined and demonstrated how to automatically make any conventional dataflow analysis able to analyze product lines in a feature-sensitive way. This way, our general idea might be used in such a work (testing) and many other areas like checking, monitoring [23], and optimizing families and product lines. For example, our feature-sensitive approach might reduce even more the time spent to figure out the relevant feature combinations of the tests.

6.6   Checking and Verification

Recent work also explored the SPL characteristics in formal modelling and verification. Vierhauser et al. [35] described experiences of applying an approach for checking consistency on variability models. Because models and the actual system tend to evolve, maintaining the consistency between them is challenging, specially when considering software families and product lines where the probability of deriving incorrect products from the models increases. They report significant performance improvements when providing feedback with respect to inconsistencies to users. In our context, development aiding tools should also provide immediate feedback for developers. We propose in this work two feature-sensitive approaches that performs better than the naive one. In addition, we provide a study that shows that the simultaneous approach is faster when compared to the consecutive. This way, we believe that the performance gains we illustrate in this work could be helpful for tools that rely on dataflow analysis and need to take features into consideration, so that they can respond quickly due to any developer action.

Classen et al. [10] shows that behavioral models offer little or no means to relate different products and their respective behavioral descriptions. In addition, they cannot use feature model information such as mutually exclusive features. To minimize these limitations, they present a transition system that takes features into consideration, so they can describe combined behavior of an entire product line. In addition, they provide a model checking technique supported by a tool capable of verifying properties for all products. Like our work, they claim that checking all product combinations instead of each product separately is faster. In particular, their model checking algorithm was on average 3.5 times faster than verifying products separately.

References

1. Aldrich, J.: Open modules: modular reasoning about advice. In: Proceedings of the 19th European Conference on Object-Oriented Programming (ECOOP), pp. 144–168. Springer (2005)
2. Alves, V., Matos, P. Jr., Cole, L., Borba, P., Ramalho, G.: Extracting and evolving mobile games product lines. In: Proceedings of the 9th International Software Product Line Conference (SPLC), of Lecture Notes in Computer Science, vol. 3714, pp. 70–81. Springer (2005)
3. Anastasopoulos, M., Muthig, D.: An evaluation of aspect-oriented programming as a product line implementation technology. In: Proceedings of the 8th International Conference on Software Reuse (ICSR). Lecture Notes in Computer Science, pp. 141–156. Springer (2004)
4. Andrade, R., Ribeiro, M., Gasiunas, V., Satabin, L., Rebelo, H., Borba, P.: Assessing idioms for implementing features with flexible binding times. In: Proceedings of the 15th European Conference on Software Maintenance and Reengineering (CSMR), pp. 231–240, IEEE Computer Society (2011)
5. Apel, S., Batory, D.: When to use features and aspects? A case study. In: Proceedings of the 5th International Conference on Generative Programming and Component Engineering (GPCE), pp. 59–68, ACM Press (2006)
6. ArgoUML. Argouml (2009), http://argouml.tigris.org/
7. Baniassad, E.L.A., Murphy, G.C.: Conceptual module querying for software reengineering. In: Proceedings of the 20th International Conference on Software Engineering (ICSE), pp. 64–73, IEEE Computer Society (1998)
8. Batory, D.S.: Feature-oriented programming and the AHEAD tool suite. In: Proceedings of the 26th International Conference on Software Engineering (ICSE), pp. 702–703, IEEE Computer Society (2004)
9. Chakravarthy, V., Regehr, J., Eric, E.: Edicts: implementing features with flexible binding times. In: Proceedings of the 7th International Conference on Aspect-Oriented Software Development (AOSD), pp. 108–119, ACM (2008)
10. Classen A., Heymans, P., Schobbens, P.-Y., Legay, A., Raskin, J.-F.: Model checking lots of systems: efficient verification of temporal properties in software product lines. In: Proceedings of the 32nd International Conference on Software Engineering (ICSE), pp. 335–344, ACM (2010)
11. Couto, M.V., Valente, M.T., Figueiredo, E.: Extracting software product lines: a case study using conditional compilation. In: Proceedings of the 15th European Conference on Software Maintenance and Reengineering (CSMR), pp. 191–200, IEEE Computer Society (2011)
12. Delaware, B., Cook, W.R., Batory, D.S.: Fitting the pieces together: a machine-checked model of safe composition. In: Proceedings of the 7th Joint Meeting of the European Software

Engineering Conference and the International Symposium on Foundations of Software Engineering (ESEC/FSE), pp. 243–252, ACM (2009)

13. Ernst, M.D., Badros, G.J., Notkin, D.: An empirical analysis of c preprocessor use. IEEE Trans. Softw. Eng. **28**, 1146–1170 (2002)

14. Feigenspan, J., Kästner, C., Apel, S., Liebig, J., Schulze, M., Dachselt, R., Papendieck, M., Leich, T., Saake, G.: Do background colors improve program comprehension in the #ifdef hell? Empir. Softw. Eng. (2012)

15. Griswold, W.G., Sullivan, K., Song, Y., Shonle, M., Tewari, N., Cai, Y., Rajan, H.: Modular software design with crosscutting interfaces. IEEE Softw. **23**(1), 51–60 (2006)

16. Horie, M., Chiba, S.: Aspectscope: an outline viewer for aspectJ programs. J. Object Technol. **6**(9), 341–361 (2007)

17. Kästner, C., Apel, S., Kuhlemann, M.: Granularity in software product lines. In: Proceedings of the 30th International Conference on Software Engineering (ICSE), pp. 311–320, ACM (2008)

18. Kästner, C., Apel, S.: Type-checking software product lines—a formal approach. In: Proceedings of the 23rd International Conference on Automated Software Engineering (ASE), pp. 258–267, IEEE Computer Society (2008)

19. Kersten, M., Murphy, G.C.: Using task context to improve programmer productivity. In: Proceedings of the 14th International Symposium on Foundations of Software Engineering (FSE), pp. 1–11, ACM (2006)

20. Kiczales, G., Mezini, M.: Aspect-oriented programming and modular reasoning. In: Proceedings of the 27th International Conference on Software Engineering (ICSE), pp. 49–58, ACM Press (2005)

21. Kiczales, G., Hilsdale, E., Hugunin, J., Kersten, M., Palm, J., Griswold, W.G.: Getting started with aspect J. Commun. ACM **44**(10), 59–65 (2001)

22. Kim, C.H., Batory, D., Khurshid, S.: Reducing combinatorics in testing product lines. In: Proceeding of the 10th International Conference on Aspect-Oriented Software Development (AOSD), pp. 57–68, ACM (2011)

23. Kim, C.H.P., Bodden, E., Batory, D., Khurshid, S.: Reducing configurations to monitor in a software product line. In: Proceedings of the 1st International Conference on Runtime Verification (RV), of Lecture Notes in Computer Science, vol. 6418, Springer (2010)

24. Laddad, R.: AspectJ in Action: Practical Aspect-Oriented Programming. Manning Publications Co. (2003)

25. LaToza, T.D., Myers, B.A.: Developers ask reachability questions. In: Proceedings of the 32nd International Conference on Software Engineering (ICSE), pp. 185–194, ACM (2010)

26. Le, D., Walkingshaw, E., Erwig, M.: #ifdef confirmed harmful: promoting understandable software variation. In: Proceedings of the International Symposium on Visual Languages and Human-Centric Computing (VL/HCC), pp. 143–150, IEEE Computer Society (2011)

27. Liebig, J., Apel, S., Lengauer, C., Kästner, C., Schulze, M.: An analysis of the variability in forty preprocessor-based software product lines. In: Proceedings of the 32nd International Conference on Software Engineering (ICSE), pp. 105–114, ACM (2010)

28. Liebig, J., Kästner, C., Apel, S.: Analyzing the discipline of preprocessor annotations in 30 million lines of C code. In: Proceeding of the 10th International Conference on Aspect-Oriented Software Development (AOSD), pp. 191–202, ACM (2011)

29. Murphy, G.C., Lai, A., Walker, R.J., Robillard, M.P.: Separating features in source code: an exploratory study. In: Proceedings of the 23rd International Conference on Software Engineering (ICSE), pp. 275–284, IEEE Computer Society (2001)

30. Ribeiro, M., Borba, P.: Improving guidance when restructuring variabilities in software product Lines. In: Proceedings of the 13th European Conference on Software Maintenance and Reengineering (CSMR), pp. 79–88, IEEE Computer Society (2009)

31. Soares, S., Laureano, E., Borba, P.: Implementing distribution and persistence aspects with aspectJ. In: Proceedings of the 17th Conference on Object-Oriented Programming, Systems, Languages and Applications (OOPSLA), pp. 174–190, ACM (2002)

32. Störzer, M., Koppen, C.: Pcdiff: attacking the fragile pointcut problem, abstract. In: Proceedings of European Interactive Workshop on Aspects in Software (2004)

33. Thaker, S., Batory, D.S., Kitchin, D., Cook, W.R.: Safe composition of product lines. In: Proceedings of the 6th International Conference Generative Programming and Component Engineering, (GPCE), pp. 95–104, ACM (2007)
34. Tip, F.: A Survey of Program Slicing Techniques. Technical report, Amsterdam, The Netherlands (1994)
35. Vierhauser, M., Grünbacher, P., Egyed, A., Rabiser, R., Heider, W.: Flexible and scalable consistency checking on product line variability models. In: Proceedings of the International Conference on Automated Software Engineering (ASE), pp. 63–72, ACM (2010)
36. Weiser, M.: Program slicing. In: Proceedings of the 5th International Conference on Software Engineering (ICSE), pp. 439–449, IEEE Press (1981)

Chapter 7
Concluding Remarks

Abstract In this chapter we point out the main aspects of our work and draw the final considerations. We summarize the work and then we present the limitations. Last but not least, we present and discuss the future work.

Keywords Interfaces · Separation of concerns · Modularity · Preprocessors · Dataflow analysis · JML · Aspect-oriented programming

This work introduced the emergent feature modularization concept to support developers when maintaining features. Although we focus on preprocessor-based families and product lines throughout this work, this concept is more general and we intend to apply it for other mechanisms like aspects. All we need to do is to compute feature dependencies on demand. Then, we emerge interfaces—developers do not need to write them—to provide information about other features we might impact with our maintenance, supporting developers when performing such a maintenance. Our interfaces abstract details from features that are not relevant to the current task, but at the same time provide valuable information to maintain a feature and keep the other ones safe. This is consistent with previous research [4]: "If all such potential 'influenced code' is clearly presented to developers, they may have better chances to detect the errors".

We presented three scenarios that can introduce errors due to such dependencies. Then, to analyze how often the feature dependency problem might occur in practice, we collected data from 43 preprocessor-based software families and product lines of different domains, sizes, and languages. The data correspond to preprocessor usage and feature dependencies frequency within methods. Basically, our results show that feature dependencies are indeed quite common in practice, giving relevance to the problem we address in this thesis.

Given the problem dimension, we presented an algorithm to compute Emergent Interfaces to address the problem. The algorithm is based on feature-sensitive dataflow analysis. In this context, we provided two approaches for taking *intraprocedural* dataflow analysis and automatically lifting it into a feature-sensitive analysis capable of analyzing all method variants. The first one (*consecutive feature sensitive*) analyses all method variants one at a time; and the second one (*simultaneous feature sensitive*) analyses all method variants at the same time.

To support developers with Emergent Interfaces, we presented Emergo, a tool capable of computing such interfaces. Therefore, after selecting the maintenance points, it computes and shows Emergent Interfaces to the developer, keeping her informed about the contracts between the selected feature and the other ones.

Besides, we performed an empirical study to evaluate the impact that feature dependencies may cause to maintenance effort using proxy metrics, which means that we measure effort indirectly. Our entire evaluation focuses only on *intraprocedural* dependencies and has three replications. Emergent Interfaces achieved effort reduction in $35.25 \pm 3.6\,\%$ of the methods we studied. We observed that the more significative reduction happens specially on methods with many fragments.

Despite the promising results, we did not evaluate many other interesting scenarios. For example, we did not consider the scalability of Emergent Interfaces when taking many other kinds of dependencies into account. Indeed, we focused on dependencies regarding only local variables, which is definitely not enough to promote full modular support when maintaining features. To compute different dependencies and thus increase the representativeness of Emergent Interfaces, we need to execute much more powerful analyses, which might lead to the performance issue we pointed out. In addition, another scalability problem arises in this context: we need to evaluate the feasibility of visualizing big interfaces. Our intuition is that dealing with (many) computed dependencies seems better than searching for them from scratch. Nevertheless, this is an important issue and we intend to investigate it as future work (see Sect. 7.2).

We also evaluated feature-sensitive approaches with respect to performance. Experimental evaluation shows that both feature-sensitive approaches are faster than the naive feature-oblivious analysis developers currently have to rely on. We also provided empirical evidence that the simultaneous is faster than the consecutive for systems with high feature usage, despite using more memory.

Finally, we claim that, in this work we provide partial feature modularization. We improve modularity by using tool-based ideas, but they are not enough. We still need language-based constructs to have characteristics such as module units and contracts to connect these units (or a set of units), allowing flexibility and changeability during maintenance tasks. Besides, Emergent Interfaces can benefit of these language constructs to improve expressiveness. For instance, we can extract information from code asserts and annotations based on languages such as Java Modeling Language (JML) [2].

7.1 Limitations

Our work has several limitations:

- The notion of feature dependency we consider takes only simple, chain of assignments and *interprocedural* into consideration;
- Our approach depends on performance and precision. This way, Emergo must respond fast. To do so, sometimes we need to compromise precision; consequently,

we might miss important feature dependencies. So, when using imprecise analyses, the use of Emergo could lead developers to a dangerous sense of security;

- We use only dataflow analysis to capture dependencies. There are, however, other techniques we could use to capture dependencies like class attribute definitions/their uses and method definitions/method calls. To do so, we might navigate throughout the AST;
- There are other kinds of dependencies we could consider by using dataflow analysis, but we neglect. For instance, we could also use dataflow analysis to capture dependencies for exception handling;
- We did not evaluate the scalability of our approach in case of having big interfaces with so many information about feature dependencies;
- The script tool to compute how often dependencies might occur in practice considers only simple dependencies and do not take dataflow analysis into account;
- The simultaneous feature-sensitive analysis does not *share* lattice values for configurations that have not yet been distinguished by the analysis, increasing memory consumption [1];
- Our performance evaluation considers only *intraprocedural* analysis. This is an important limitation because the performance issue seems to appear only for *interprocedural* dependencies (although we did not notice during our experiments any overhead that would make our approach not viable). Evaluating the performance of *interprocedural* analyses is important to define a balance between precision and performance. In addition, our evaluation does not use statistical tests. So, we do not analyze the statistic significance of the time differences.

7.2 Future Work

In particular, we intend to complement this work with the following future work:

- Despite focusing on preprocessor-based families and product lines, the emergent feature modularization concept is general. We illustrate in Sect. 4.8 we can use Emergent Interfaces in other mechanisms, such as aspects. Therefore, we intend to design, implement, and evaluate Emergent Interfaces using such a mechanism;
- In this book, we focus on software *maintenance*. We also intend to design, implement, and evaluate Emergent Interfaces to focus on software *development*. In particular, we also intend to enable parallel development using our technique;
- Formalize the computation of Emergent Interfaces by considering contracts;
- We also intend to perform additional work towards better understanding feature code dependencies in preprocessor-bases families and product lines [3];
- To improve the representativeness of Emergent Interfaces, we intend to consider different kinds of feature dependencies, which require different analyses and a performance evaluation in this scenario. After computing them, we need to evaluate the scalability of our approach. For example, we intend to evaluate the feasibility of visualizing big Emergent Interfaces.

References

1. Brabrand, C., Ribeiro, M., Tolêdo, T., Borba, P.: Intraprocedural dataflow analysis for software product lines. In: Proceedings of the 11th International Conference on Aspect-Oriented Software Development (AOSD), pp. 13–24. ACM (2012)
2. Leavens, G.T., Baker, A.L., Ruby, C.: Preliminary design of JML: a behavioral interface specification language for Java. SIGSOFT Softw. Eng. Not. **31**(3), 1–38 (2006)
3. Queiroz, F., Ribeiro, M., Soares, S., Borba, P.: Towards a better understanding of feature dependencies in preprocessor-based systems. In: Proceedings of the 6th Latin American Workshop on Aspect-Oriented Software Development: Advanced Modularization Techniques (LA-WASP) (2012)
4. Yin, Z., Yuan, D., Zhou, Y., Pasupathy, S., Bairavasundaram, L.: How do fixes become bugs? In: Proceedings of the 19th ACM SIGSOFT Symposium and the 13th European Conference on Foundations of Software Engineering (ESEC/FSE), pp. 26–36. ACM (2011)